T

9

TITANIA'S NUMBER 9

Titania Hardie

CONNECTIONS
BOOK PUBLISHING

For Carolyn Elfin-queen, darling Dottie, and baby Remy!

A CONNECTIONS EDITION
This edition published in Great Britain in 2007 by
Connections Book Publishing Limited
St Chad's House, 148 King's Cross Road, London WC1X 9DH
www.connections-publishing.com

British Library Cataloguing-in-Publication data available on request.

ISBN 978-1-85906-231-9

1   3   5   7   9   10   8   6   4   2

Phototypeset in Bliss and Natural Script using QuarkXPress on Apple Macintosh
Printed in China

Contents

STARTING THE JOURNEY

This little book of numerology invites you to be amazed by what you will learn from numbers – about your character, your tastes, your instincts, your relationships, and even about your future. But to do this involves a willingness to believe – as Pythagoras, the 'Father of Numbers' did – that numbers can provide a clue, or formula, through which we can perceive some of the evolving patterns and cycles that affect our own individual existence.
Let's find out more ...

Discovering numerology

Fans of Sudoku will understand how it entices us intellectually to see how strands of numbers – almost magically – slot together and interconnect with one another, revealing a rhythm of harmonious relationships between the lines. In one sense, numerology does this for us on a personal and spiritual level. The Science of Numbers, as it is called, suggests that there is an order and a rhythm in the universe of which we are a part, and although there is a certain mystery in the way numbers seem to function as symbols for our experiences, there is a long tradition across many cultures of their fascination for us.

Now, in an age of gigabytes, PINs and mathematic-based technology, how can we doubt the role that numbers play, or the way in which they have become part of our daily landscape? Numbers speak to us every day about

8   7   6   5   4   3   2   1   9

our personal identity on this planet. Our birth date is absorbed by society as proof of our existence: you need it to be 'real' at the bank, in the office, when you travel, in an automated phone queue – in *all* official records. Indeed, many people consider the day-date of their birth-day to be their lucky number. But can it really say anything about us?

Did you know, for instance, that:

- If you were a **5**, you'd need to invest in good-quality luggage because you'd be bound to notch up a lot of air miles?
- Or that a **4** will painstakingly spend hours getting something just right, whereas a **1** will rush in and get several projects started, full of enthusiasm, only to leave someone else to carry them through to completion?
- Or that a **7** will want to specialize in whatever is of particular interest to them?

| 9 | 1 | 2 | 3 | 4 | 5 | 6 | 7 | 8 |

- And a **3** is a born entertainer, who enjoys sharing time with others, whereas a **2** prefers to live quietly, with just one or two partnerships, both socially and in business?

But you've picked *this* little volume because you're a **9**, traveller and genial raconteur with a hundred friends who all visit regularly to watch you play host. An **8**, on the other hand, is the spendthrift soul who will take *everyone* to lunch on their bill, while a **6** prefers to cook quietly at home for their extended family.

About this book

Each individual title in this series investigates, in depth, the meaning of one of nine personal numbers. *This* volume is dedicated to the exploration of the number **9**.

We will be focusing principally on your **DAY** number — that is, the number relating to the day of the month on which you were born (in your case, the 9th, 18th or 27th of the month) Calculating your **DAY** number is easy: you simply add the digits of your day together (where applicable), and keep adding them until they reduce to a single number (*see calculation examples on page 270*). And that's it. It doesn't matter which month or year you were born in – you just need the day-date to discover your **DAY** number. And *you're* a **9**.

Your **DAY** number reveals all kinds of information, and, working from this number, we will be considering:

- The obvious attributes of your number as they impact on your personality
- How you are likely to dress, and what colours or styles appeal
- How you react to things psychologically, and what drives or motivates you
- What annoys you most

9   1   2   3   4   5   6   7   8

- In which fields you will have the most natural abilities and gifts
- What sort of lover you are, and how you relate to all other numbers
- What the future holds

... and much, much more.

And you have another significant number too: your LIFE number. This is derived from adding up the digits in the *whole* of your birth date – day, month and year (*see examples on page 270*). What does *this* number mean, and what do your DAY and LIFE numbers mean in tandem? And how does it affect you if you're also a 'master' number (**11** or **22**)? Read on and you'll see. But first, let's meet your DAY number ...

8   7   6   5   4   3   2   1   9

So, you're a 9

9

As a **9**, you have seen it all before: yours is the number of **wisdom**, and your **life's experience** contributes towards an attitude of forgiveness. **9** is a 'mirror' number, reflecting all people and experiences in its own eyes. It symbolizes universal brotherhood and **idealism**, and sometimes a sense of **sadness** and moodiness surrounds your number, too. At home, **9** is the clown and the **actor**, playing out various roles, mimicking and **feeling** for others. You **absorb** everything you become exposed to – for both good and ill; though you would like to hope for the best in everyone, you probably know better.

To make you wise before your time and **kind** to others, you may experience many disappointments in life and feel

| 9 | 1 | 2 | 3 | 4 | 5 | 6 | 7 | 8 |

the **winds of change** from your childhood. Security is often the most elusive thing for you, and your family and upbringing may have forced you to become **personally adaptable**. This is true also for your later life, when circumstances alter readily – and yet you **cope** with whatever is hurled at you with grace. Your number is nevertheless exceptionally friendly, **broad-thinking**, well-read, and you may look on the whole world as part of your personal playground. **9** is not fenced in, and thinks of the full measure of time and place constantly, throughout life. This is why yours is the number of **travel**.

A **9**'s close parental bond is with the father, but this may well have come about because your father was absent or busy in your early life, leaving you feeling a huge but unfulfilled **longing** relating to him. Or, in some cases, the father may be missing altogether, and you must search out a true image of him in your imagination. This can mean you feel **loss**, or that the father becomes

8 7 6 5 4 3 2 1 9

the idolized parent. A **9**'s father is never merely a lukewarm person in their life.

9 is a **clairvoyant** and **highly intuitive** number because it mirrors all other numbers: any number that is added to it reduces back to the original number (for example: 5+9 = 14, and 1+4 = 5). You absorb other people's feelings, **reflecting** them back for others to see. **9** is thus an actor, but also a wise **counsellor**. You see the need for separations and **endings** when other numbers will struggle on in an attempt to defy the inevitable. You won't necessarily enjoy these truths, but you see the shape of how it must be, so you receive special – possibly divine – **help** and **protection** to get you through these unusual experiences.

Your talents are so manifold – not necessarily a good thing. Your excellent **imagination** and ability to **empathize** gives you exactly the right skills to act, paint and write professionally. Theatre, in fact, is a fruitful field

9   1   2   3   4   5   6   7   8

for **9**s, because all your talents can be used under one roof. **9**s also feel a lust for travel, and if your actual business is not travel itself, your work life will probably incorporate travel in some sense. Other talents include music, PR, lecturing, heading a sales force, reading and writing for work, and IT at the superior level.

In love relationships, your immense **charm** and true-life experiences make you very popular and **much desired**; you seem to have done a great deal by the time you're in your late teens, and have **many facets** to your character. You need a **positive** love partner, because your tendency to absorb the moods of whomever is close dictates a need to be careful in depressed company: you would be plummeting right alongside anyone who is very low all the time. Also, someone who understands your will to constantly disappear off into your head, **wandering**, thinking and reflecting, is vital. In relationships you often can't help **creating changes** – which are part of your nature

and experience – so you may have a few false starts before
you finally find the one to last.

*Sound familiar? Getting a taste for what your
number is about? And this is just the beginning.
You'll soon find out how the number 9 expresses
itself as your Day number in each and every day
of your life. But before we go any further, let's
take a look at where all this first came from …*

What's in a number?

Numbers have always had a sacred meaning. The Egyptians used an alphabet that conflated letters and numbers, and, as such, each number exuded an idea that was more than the sum it stood for. There is a whole book of the Old Testament devoted to the subject; and the Hebrew language – exactly like the Egyptian – has a magical subtext of meaning where letters and numbers can be doubled to reveal an extra layer of secret, so-called 'occult' information. It is called the *gematria*, and forms a crucial part of the sacred occult wisdom called Kabbalah. There were twenty-two letters – a master number – in both the Greek (Phoenician) and Hebrew alphabets, and repetitions of the spiritual properties of the numbers **3** and, especially, **7** recur throughout the Bible.

8   7   6   5   4   3   2   1   9

The Father of Numbers

But modern numerology derives more formally from Pythagoras, the Father of Numbers, who was a serious and spiritual philosopher, as well as the man who explained some of the secrets of geometry. Born on the island of Samos, although he ultimately settled in Cretona, a Greek colony in southern Italy, he is understood to have travelled widely to both Egypt and Judea. Some accounts of his life also suggest he may have studied under the Persian sages of Zoroaster, but an analysis of his teachings certainly reveals the strong influence of Kabbalistic thought in his philosophy.

Pythagoras understood numbers as a *quality* of being, as well as a *quantity* of material value. In one sense, the numbers as figures were connected with the measuring of things, but 'number' itself was significantly different to this, and encompassed a spiritual value. The numbers from

9 1 2 3 4 5 6 7 8

one through to nine represented universal principles through which everything evolves, symbolizing even the stages an idea passes through before it becomes a reality. Mathematics was the tool through which we could apprehend the Creation, the universe, and ourselves. Musical harmony was a sacred part of this knowledge, as was geometry, which revealed divine proportion.

Most importantly, Pythagoras believed that numbers were expressive of the principles of all real existence – that numbers themselves embodied the principles of our dawning awareness, our conjecture and growth. Through mathematics and number we could approach divine wisdom and the workings of the universe as a macrocosm. Thus, in microcosm, our personal 'mathematics' would unlock the workings of our own being, and help us to see a divine wisdom concerning ourselves. **1** was not just the first digit, but also had a character of beginning, of independence, of leadership, just as the number **2** was more than merely the second number quantifying two objects, but also implied the philosophical concept of a pair, of co-operation, of a relationship beyond the individual.

Pythagoras also believed that we could understand our direction and fate through an awareness of repeating cycles of number, making numerology a key to revealing our opportunities and our destiny.

By tradition, the doctrine Pythagoras taught to his students in the sixth century BCE was secret, and no one wrote down his ideas until his death. But Plato was a follower of Pythagoras and, along with the rebirth of Platonism, the ideas of the Father of Mathematics were revealed afresh during the revival of Greek learning in the Renaissance. The great magi of the fifteenth and sixteenth centuries explored anew the significance of number and the gematria, to understand the hidden messages of the ancients and of the divine mind. Mathematics as a philos-ophy was the bridge to higher realms of spirituality.

9　1　2　3　4　5　6　7　8

Essence of the numbers

one is the spark, the beginning, Alpha, the Ego of consciousness. It is male.

two is consort. Adding partnership, receptivity, it is female, bringing tact.

three is a synthesizing of both of these qualities and brings expansion and joy.

four is the number of the Earth, of the garden, and of stability. It brings order.

five is curiosity and experiment, freedom, changes. It brings sensuality.

six nurtures and cares for others. It will love and beautify, and brings counsel.

seven perfects and contemplates the Creation. It is intellect, stillness, spirit.

eight is the number of power, the octave, a higher incarnation. It brings judgement.

nine is humanity, selflessness, often impersonal and all-knowing. It brings compassion.

8 7 6 5 4 3 2 1 9

Applying the knowledge

A deeper understanding of the self can be achieved through an awareness of the mysticism of number within us; and both the birth date and, to some degree, our given name are the keys to unlocking our mystical, spiritual core of being. Exploring the affinity between letter and number can also reveal insights about the lessons we need to learn throughout our lives to improve and develop as individuals (*see page 25*).

This book looks at the significance of numbers as they affect us every day, focusing largely, as introduced earlier, on our **DAY** number. It is this number that reveals to us our instincts, our impulses, our natural tastes and undiluted responses, our talents and immediate inclina-tions. This is how people see us in daily situations, and how we behave by essence.

We will be exploring how our **DAY** number influences

9   1   2   3   4   5   6   7   8

our love relationships and friendships; at what it says about our career strengths and our childhood; at the way our number manifests in our leisure time; and at how it might give us a better understanding of what to expect in our future cycles, as we pass through any given year under the sway of a particular number. Each birthday initiates a new cycle, and each cycle seems uncannily connected with the philosophical concerns of the number which governs that year. Look both to the past and present to see how strongly the number-cycle can illuminate our experiences ... and then count ahead to ponder what may be in store over the next year or two.

And numbers also say something about where we live or work, about our car, and even about our pets. Understanding these secret qualities can add a new dimension of pleasure – not to mention surprise – to our journey through life.

8 7 6 5 4 3 2 1 9

A NUMBER TO GROW INTO

The presence of our LIFE number, however, takes longer for us to appreciate in ourselves – longer for us to grow into – and it often takes time to reveal itself. This number comes to the fore as your life progresses, and on pages 214–247 we will be looking at the meaning of your DAY number together with your individual LIFE number, to see what this reveals about your character and potentiality.

The LIFE number may intensify the experience of the DAY number – if it is closely related to it, or shares similar patterns. But more frequently our two different numbers clash a little, and this often allows insight into the aspects of our being where instinct pulls us in one direction but higher wisdom or experience mediates and pulls us in a second direction.

Who would have thought you could learn so much from a number? Pythagoras certainly did, over 2,500 years ago ... and now you will discover it too.

9   1   2   3   4   5   6   7   8

What's in a name?

Your name also has a story to tell, and it is a story revealed through number. Every letter corresponds to a number: in the Western alphabet we use twenty-six letters, which are at variance with the twenty-two formerly enshrined in the Hebrew and Greek alphabets. Some numerologists believe that this is in keeping with the more material world we now live in, as the number '26' reduces to '8' (when you add the digits), which is the number of power and money.

The correspondences between the numbers and the letters of the alphabet are as follows:

1	2	3	4	5	6	7	8	9
A	B	C	D	E	F	G	H	I
J	K	L	M	N	O	P	Q	R
S	T	U	V	W	X	Y	Z	

8	7	6	5	4	3	2	1	9

As you are a **9**, it is most revealing to look at the letters I and R as they occur (or not!) in your name. This is because they intensify the experience and impression of your main number.

To make the most of the qualities inherent in your number, you should be using a name which is in poetic harmony with your **DAY** number. As a **9**, you prefer to see things through to completion, and you will weave the most fruitful blend of unique talents if you have a name which underlines your strongly diverse **9** qualities. Using a name which includes an I or an R bolsters your powers. If this sounds strange, consider that many of us have our names shortened or played upon by friends, family and lovers, so it is important to feel that our chosen name – the one that we use as we go about in the world – is making the best of our abilities and energies.

Among the letters that are equivalent to the number **9**, R is a relatively common consonant – so the chances are that you have this letter in your name. Also, I is a common vowel, and if your name begins with one of these two letters, or if the first vowel in your name is I, it strengthens the power of your number **9** right at the beginning of your name. Create a nickname or pet name with it in, if necessary, to back up the outstanding properties of creativity that come with your number.

The letter-numbers help us to act out our sense of purpose, and if these work in correspondence with the DAY number we are more likely to find our sense of will and achieve our goals more rapidly. But if we have few, or none, of the letters of our DAY number, we often feel it is much harder to shine in our field of opportunity.

Missing a '9' letter?

As a **9**, you rely on communicating well with others, but if you have no '**9**' letters in your name you may need to

8   7   6   5   4   3   2   1   9

develop your confidence and your broader thinking, as well as your feelings of compassion for others.

You may still be a dreamer with the strongest ideas about what will make a better world, and yet feel a block to realizing your wishes. Also, your career may frustrate your creativity. A '**9**' letter added into your name – perhaps as a company or a pet name, or by playing with the spelling of your name – will help you gain confidence about the way the world sees and responds to you, and give you more optimism about your personal relationships.

Too many 'R's and 'I's?

It can be just as much of a problem if your name carries a flood of letters which correspond to your number. Where a lack of 'R's could make you unsure of how to use your philosophical and altruistic instincts to their best advantage, a surfeit could make you a bit too headstrong and a

| 9 | 1 | 2 | 3 | 4 | 5 | 6 | 7 | 8 |

law unto yourself. Too many 'R's could also make you rush your fences and act rashly, while too many 'I's (more than three) contributes to very intensely felt emotions and a lack of objectivity.

Work to balance your fine feelings and energies, and guard against burn-out. You may need to reduce the number of 'I's or 'R's you use in your everyday or business name. But the **9** letters are certainly artistic, and if your first vowel is an I, you may be a gifted writer or good with a sewing needle; you are also highly intuitive and very sympathetic with others. '**9**' letters (in moderation) help you finish what you start.

YOUR DAY NUMBER
It's a new day ...

You will learn a lot about the numbers of your birthday and your name as this book unfolds, but the DAY number is, to my mind, the most important – and sometimes least well-recognized – number of all ... the number which exerts a magnetic hold on us each and every day of our lives. Every time we react to a situation, an emotion, a provocation of any kind, we are shooting straight from the hip, as it were, and this reaction is coloured by our DAY number.

| 9 | 1 | 2 | 3 | 4 | 5 | 6 | 7 | 8 |

As we know, your 'Day Force', or DAY, number is **9** if you were born on the 9th, 18th or 27th of any month. Each of these different dates also affects us – the characteristics of the number derived from a birthday on the 18th vary intriguingly from one on the 27th, for instance – and we will look at these differences in the pages ahead.

All three dates, however, still reconcile to an overall **9**. This number determines your gut reactions and the way you express yourself when you are being most true to yourself. Your parents, lovers, friends and co-workers all know you best through this number.

So what is the theme of being a 9? What are you like when you're at work, rest and play? And how compatible are you with the other numbers? Let's find out ...

8   7   6   5   4   3   2   1   9

9'S CHARACTER
Charms, graces, warts and all ...

This is truly a number given to the soul who will seek a certain level of mastery of life – even if, at times, it seems that the world expects just too much from you. Your number is sensitive to the music of the spheres in its most artistic and intellectual applications; you are alert to the possibility of one divine mind, one universal spirit, one harmonious creation. 9 is the number of higher love and wisdom; your number yearns to educate others, open their minds, and bring music to their ears. This number asks that you give service to others, but personal happiness need not be elusive as long as you balance your individual wishes alongside the call to be charitable and good.

9 1 2 3 4 5 6 7 8

The tests of time

As the final single-figure digit – with only master numbers **11** and **22** to supersede it – **9** is the number of completion and attainment. The striving for personal perfection may become an obsession, because you want to make things better than they have been for your family, your friends and for the brotherhood of the human race. Disappointments must inevitably come when you have such a push to high achievement, but there is compensation for this, because you will come to feel truly appreciated and looked up to as your life unfolds. Time is a friend to the number **9**, and as you move in the widest circles and across the greatest plateaus of activity and experience, everything becomes more vivid and rewarding. For a **9**, middle age is the beginning of the greatest scope and joy.

From your childhood, you have faced tests and personal demands – partly to put other people first, and to

8   7   6   5   4   3   2   1   9

erase any inclination towards selfishness. This is a maturing task for a young person, and thus **9** may be either the eldest sibling, who looks after the younger ones, or the youngest, who fits in after everyone else's wishes have been attended to. You learn, from necessity, to be tolerant about those less capable or broad-minded than you; and you discover tactics for deflecting the anger and over-sensitivity of other people.

It takes some time for the most important people around you to understand your sympathetic, tactful nature, and this requires patience from you. But **9** is a quick learner and inclined to a philosophical disposition, which helps. You also take comfort in certain things others can't even reach. Books, travel, theatre and world affairs are bread-and-butter interests for **9**, and you will always find inspiration in a leaf or a flower if you need it. You are a person of deep resources.

Keynotes of the 9 personality

Positive associations: broad thinker, creative imagination,
lover of variety, perfectionist, idealist, charitable,
forgiving, lucky with money, kind, spiritual (perhaps even
conventionally religious), dramatic and artistic talents

Negative associations: can be changeable and moody
(especially in love), often possessive about love ties, hot-
headed, careless about friends and finances, difficulty
focusing energies, too many personal interests and affairs

Guiding light

Whether your interest lies in local authority and social
activity or in the bigger, wiser (often foreign) world, you will
come to know a great many people of influence. You have
an instinct to protect those who need you – making you an
attentive parent or a superb counsellor – but **9** is more concerned with the underdog than the victor. A philanthropist,

8   7   6   5   4   3   2   1   9

your generosity of spirit is marked. Always thinking of others, to the point where your personal life suffers, you have a desire for freedom from bigotry and meanness that makes you something of a light for others to follow. At times, the pressure of this role can be immense, but by reaching out to the larger world, you will rally.

With so much asked of you in the social world, you have been given great gifts. Deep intuition, a feeling imagination and significant intellectual powers come to a **9**. Add to this the fact that at various times you may be lucky with money and with friends, with opportunities and with invitations, and others will look up to you as an ideal and wise-minded being. When you turn your charms on anyone, you are impossible to deny.

You can be, and may be expected to be, blessed with largesse of nature that enables you to rise above all the pettiness and prickliness you find in others about you. You can understand and forgive lesser souls their selfishness

9   1   2   3   4   5   6   7   8

and narrower motives, and rise above niggling situations. Even when you suffer sorrow and loss, you will try to view the wider picture, and to put your own pain into perspective with the greater world. It is an astonishing capacity, and one that ultimately brings you divine protection if you are open to it. In fact, it is just because you learn across the years to love life and to attract success in an impersonal way – without the need for individual prominence or accolade – that so much is lauded upon you. It is your just deserts for a generous nature.

Get the balance right

But all is not a continuously rosy path for **9**. During your early life and while you are studying and training, tests of your generosity – and your resolve – often arise. You may be rich one day and impoverished the next, making, losing and rebuilding your finances time and again. With a 'live

8   7   6   5   4   3   2   1   9

and let live' attitude, you aren't focused on accumulating either funds or honours or fame; friends are your riches, and you are too giving in your nature to hoard what you earn.

On the other hand, you are destined to live and see life, so opportunities to do this may arise in a variety of ways. It takes some years to discover the way to be of use to others, generous to their needs, without incurring personal loss. In the intervening time, you will discover an ability to recover – no matter how harsh the odds – and to restore your name or lifestyle. You have exceptional talents – artistically, intellectually and emotionally – and, when you can understand how to bring them into balance, you should discover both success and security.

Letting go

One of the most demanding strains placed on a **9** concerns the problem of letting people go from your life. **9** is

9	1	2	3	4	5	6	7	8

the number of completion, as we said earlier, and also of endings. This often forces you to move on, and away from those who are no longer moving in the same true direction as you are, and many relationships fall by the wayside over the course of a **9**'s lifetime. It is not that you are expected to be alone, or even without a close companion; but you will often have to take stock and contemplate what is still viable, still of use to you. You must constantly grow, think and change – even if others remain static.

This does, in truth, sometimes set you apart from the crowd, forcing you to dig deep into your heart and mind for what is really important in life. These soul-searching questions help you to arrive at a singular wisdom, and it is this wise mind, in turn, which provides the material for you to write, act, create ideas of spiritual beauty. Your number is the most naturally gifted actor, the true literary spirit, the great mirror of humanity. But these are big responsibilities, of course!

Your mental and creative acuity don't stop at the normal course of artistic talents. **9** is a number that can respond to the most unusual and irregular stimuli. You can understand deep and complex people, and may have patience with those who listen to nobody else. Children with learning difficulties, or who suffer from illness, and people at odds with society's dictates – all may respond vividly to your charm and your communication skills. Your sympathy and understanding are genuine, and this is felt. You also have a rare ability to get right inside another human being's skin – to see the world through their eyes – and you are alert to sound and music with a particular sensitivity. It is this that makes you a great speaker and a warm raconteur.

Your humour has been shaped by personal adversity and joy – and recognition of the fact that pleasure is made more exquisite in contrast to pain already suffered is what keeps your feet firmly planted on the ground, and gives you the capacity to recover after hardship. You are respected and well-liked, a popular cohort or member of any business team, a good companion on a rainy day. But always remember that it is imperative for your own happiness that you allow yourself some relaxing time – in sunny company of your own. So subject to nuance and hurt, you can be too open to mopping up other people's miseries in too personal a way. Don't forget the need to balance the giving activity without the demand for personal loss; you can't help anyone if you are either exhausted or emotionally drained yourself.

Public service

When your business is destined to be concerned with service – with 'helping' the world – what might that mean for you in career terms? We will look at this in more detail in the following section but, briefly, publishing is traditionally a **9** occupation — partly because of the potential to reach so many people in so many places across the globe. You have a talent for writing and words — either as a public speaker, actor or dramatic writer, or as a politician or teacher at the top level. Like **7**, you would need to work as a lecturer or an advanced, specialist teacher. But a person with these skills might as easily enter the law, or use their creative energies and selflessness to be a great surgeon. Health is certainly of interest to **9**, as is the subject of personal spirituality and questing.

Whether you are the psychically inspired actor or the world-affairs-minded diplomat, you will have a career that asks some public duty of you in some way, and you will be called upon to 'act out' a variety of subsumed roles that come under a broader cloak. It is also highly probable that you will speak several languages — or snippets of them, at least — as **9** is truly a global traveller.

In the eye of the beholder

In personal relationships, you can have much misplaced faith in others less selfless than you who will let you down. You may have to work hard not to be overtaken by your emotions – especially hanging on to the past when it's of no use. You are attracted to beautiful people – not just physically, but in abstract ways – but you are sometimes overly romantic, and love with too great an intensity. Sometimes you must hold back a touch, and be prepared that others may not be able to live up to your high expectations. On the other hand, it's not uncommon for a **9** to have some strange love affairs, and you may startle or confuse others who have a different judgement of what is desirable.

Take care not to become compulsively self-sacrificial in relationships, for this is a recipe for pain and uncertainty. Accept that what makes you happy may divide you from others, and take joy from the cerebral and physical pleasures in the world you create around you – including your home, which will be extremely special to you.

A life less ordinary

Those negative traits – depressive tendencies, dissipation of your abilities, the possibility of turning your hand to too many things – are all potentially destructive if you let them dominate your personality or lifestyle. **9** can be too impulsive, too nervy, too demanding of others' feelings and emotional responsiveness. But this is to overstate what is a negative *possibility* – not an inevitability. You would be better summed up through your magnetism, your broad mind and charming manner towards others. **9** is a number of beauty, so your chances of having been blessed with good looks and a good heart and spirit are high.

Find the balance between collapsing with pity for every sad story and being truly selfless to a positive and useful end. Having faith and confidence in your talents and character is the starting point of living an extraordinary life. If you are shy and retiring, you haven't found your exceptional strength and inner beauty yet. But, you will.

9 in a nutshell

Personality watchwords: receptive, sensitive, idealist
Lucky colours: straw, olive green, smoke
Lucky herbs/flowers: olive, lemon-flower, lotus, sage, wormwood, willow
Scents: lemon, lime, verbena, green tea, vetiver
Fashion style: smooth, tactile, comfortable, artistic lines
Decorative style: fairly open space for entertaining, with outdoor aspect
Letters: I or R (needed in the name you use)
Car style: big enough to transport friends and family, made for mileage rather than glamour
Holiday destination: the world! (deserts, mountains, sea)

8   7   6   5   4   3   2   1   9

Which 9 are you?

5   6   7   8   **9**   1   2   3   4

Everyone with a **DAY** number of **9** will exhibit many of the characteristics just discussed. It is interesting to see, though, how the number **9** varies across all of its incarnations. There is a subtle but definite difference between the way the number operates for someone born on the 9th of the month – which makes for a pure **9** effect – and someone born, say, on the 27th.

As a rule, anyone born on the single-digit date has the truest and most undiluted effect from the number, whereas someone born as a product of two digits borrows some qualities from the pairing of the numbers. Twenty-anything puts the softening digit '2' before the second number, and this usually means that, whatever number you are, you are even more aware of the needs of others. Similarly, if '1' is the first digit (18th) you are more independent, and perhaps more assured of your self-worth, than other **9** people.

Let's look at the variations across all
the birthdays . . .

Born on the 9th?

With the purest form of **9**, yours is a lovely birthday. Patient and kind to the nth degree, your version of **9** embraces the intellectual and artistic talents of the number to the full. You love variety and change, but you care particularly deeply about seeing things through to completion. This is important, because some **9**s often suffer impulsive moods that urge them to move on before they have achieved tangible results.

You are less afraid of responsibility than other **9**s, ready to be both passionate and committed to what you believe in. You can be reached through your emotions, and you have a particularly strong humanitarian nature. A philanthropist who must be given an opportunity to express your talents before the public, you are almost certainly a gifted speaker and actor, and in everyday life you undoubt-

| 9 | 1 | 2 | 3 | 4 | 5 | 6 | 7 | 8 |

edly assume roles without even noticing you do so.

Travelling may be a regular part of your life, and you will notch up many miles if you have half a chance. Your life will be exposed to many changes, some of which are changes of location and home. You may suffer those losses and separations from family and friends we spoke of earlier, for one reason or another. Most **9**s experience this because of the amount of travel they – or loved ones – endure, and as your birthday is the pure form of **9** you may experience this more than any other **9** birthday!

It would be very unusual if you were either petty or the kind of person who takes offence easily. Others may become sidetracked by minutiae, but it is your way to see the whole picture and look at how others are also feeling. This overview makes you a good artist, and you can easily succeed in many arts-related endeavours, possessing particular literary, painting and musical skills. Your pure **9** is the mirror number, allowing you to reflect back what you see in others. You hardly seem aware of your gift for looking deeply into someone, and understanding just how they feel emotionally and psychologically; you know what they are experiencing.

Thus, this birthday is characteristic of those sensitive souls who have a striking capacity for clairvoyance, acting, and all forms of counselling. These intuitive gifts are rarely at odds with your keen intellect, and you may be drawn to genuine study and interest in the metaphysical, without feeling the pressure to be sceptical about everything. You know about spiritual matters, since you can absorb and then reflect many people's experiences as if at first hand. This may disgruntle, or amaze, those you meet.

In your career life you will need an intellectual challenge. Any area connected with film or drama, writing, travelling, teaching, law, advertising or foreign affairs will be right up your street. If you pause and consider that your greatest chance of happiness will come from helping others, there is no end to what you may achieve. Mostly, **9** is lucky with money, and you may be better able to preserve what you earn than someone born on the 18th or the 27th.

The number **9** matches the tarot card known as 'The Hermit', or 'The Sage'; and there is an aspect of this in your character, too. Here is the being who has achieved wisdom through self-sacrifice and long years lived in the mind, offering service and illumination to the world. And this also illuminates the clear need you may feel for some privacy at times.

8 7 6 5 4 3 2 1 9

Born on the 18th?

Borrowing some dynamism from the number **1** preceding the powerful **8**, a birthday on the 18th goes hand in hand with an intellectual mind and a physically active individual. Your birthday is that of the traveller, the emotional but understanding character, the **9** who needs the constant run of change in their daily affairs. You have an intense mind and strong emotions and opinions, so you can be very fond of an argument, enjoying the challenge and the sparring. You also love your independence, and easily become a leader in any group situation. This gives you extra charisma, an ability to reach the public, and you are wise when it comes to giving advice, and not shy of offering it. You receive extremely powerful impressions from your subconscious mind, and a deep intuitive response to people and places.

9   1   2   3   4   5   6   7   8

Of all the **9**s, you are the most loyal in relationships, sticking at tasks until shared jobs are completed or until the bond improves. This is despite the fact that you feel strongly pressed to make changes, but change is a separate discussion from loyalty, and you are willing to stay close to someone or something in need. Perhaps you are conservative in some of your thinking and in your business choices, but you are quite adept at handling or saving money and at making relationships work within a team. However, do try not to be too critical of others, in your drive to complete or perfect situations and ideas: not everyone learns or thinks as quickly as you. Be positive and encouraging with those who need your direction and contribution, as no one is better able to impart good advice lovingly and humorously – if you are in the mood to do so.

A lover of music and a true admirer of both theatre and literature, you may be very well-educated and well-read, even if you are largely self-taught. You have a flavour of the theatrical about you — whether you are making an entrance or finding the fitting bon mot for a meeting or a public event. Like most of the **9**s, you would undoubtedly be a good writer of true-to-life fiction or sitcom dramas.

With this birthday you may be subjected to frequent and unexpected change in both your career and your personal life, but you will admit — if you are fair — that it is your inner restlessness that often forces this change to occur. You also love the possibility of travel, and will look for opportunities to down-tools and get away. If you don't travel physically, you will travel mentally, or through books and other media — or this may even take the form of absent-minded thought, travelling away from a situation you are forced into, and escaping in the mind.

Your career will flourish in any field that offers you scope, particularly politics, because you assume the 'big brother' role towards others throughout your life. Fine art, acting and law are also excellent options for you, and you might be very drawn to medicine. Do be aware that '18' has a connection with matters of health, so guard against allowing yourself to become overly stressed or worn out mentally with career pressures. **9**, your base number, is the listener's number, and this can deplete your energies if you are also working at full stretch. Always find time for some fresh air and exercise.

Born on the 27th?

The 27th is a lovely birthday, as the '2' in the birth date gives you an extra, spiritual quality by putting other people first much of the time. You have a much broader understanding of people's feelings and their differences, and you are one of life's more unprejudiced souls. Both wise and fair, you will strive for harmony, and work to make others happier when they are under siege.

This **9** goes hand in hand with literary taste and verbal style, and you may find a tremendous opportunity to market and develop your ideas in the world. You have a fertile intellectual capacity and a very good memory, and it may be one of your priorities to bring your concepts to fruition in the real marketplace. You have an eye for beauty, good taste, and a sense of the value of making beautiful but useful products. This means that you could

9   1   2   3   4   5   6   7   8

succeed in a variety of different business enterprises, and enjoy every one of them for a different reason. Perhaps one day you will find you have arrived at personal success without ever noticing you were trying to reach it. This is not least because you have the ability to think and act independently.

Poised and reflective, you are able to understand others' feelings so personally that you grieve for anyone in pain as though they were close family. This is why you have a powerful desire to help everyone achieve happiness, physical well-being and intellectual goals. You yourself are mostly tranquil on the outside, but you can be nervous and erratic in private, where only you know how you are feeling. At peak times of work stress or family turmoil, you become more confused and indecisive, unsure of the best path to take or best impression to adhere to. You become infuriated by the weaknesses of others, but even more so by any failing in yourself. Perhaps this is because you do feel things so acutely, and you lose the objectivity your mind is otherwise so capable of. When harmony is restored, so is your excellent judgement. This is why it is best to avoid relationships – personal or business – which put you on the back foot or make you feel small and defensive.

Once you have decided on a course of action, you don't like to be challenged. You are a leader and will not enjoy working for others. You will work happily under your own direction, absorbed for hours in a complicated task, or sometimes instructing a team; you will always be a good motivator to others. Just remember to avoid burdening yourself with negative or closed people, as you know you can be deeply affected by adverse comment, and will take on their misery and lack of optimism.

Strongly developed musical, dramatic and literary abilities make you a regular on the concert and theatre run. With so many friends, you will always have a social companion, and you may even have a group you dance or sing with, or take weekend breaks with. Likely to be fascinated by the mysticism of past cultures, and strongly drawn to Eastern cultures and art, you will always feel very comfortable with metaphysical matters. You are a deeply affectionate human being, with a very unique and different take on problems and puzzles. Others seek you out in a crisis, for help finding solutions. But you may have to handle disappointments when others cannot return your generosity of time or – also – your intensity of emotion. Love affairs can be frustrating for you sometimes.

A constant traveller, you may one day elect to live abroad. Natural space and light, and a love of the sea, makes your home an important place to curl up after a long day, but avoid forcing yourself into a limiting environment domestically.

8 7 6 5 4 3 2 1 9

9 AT WORK

So, what kind of employee does your number make you? We've already seen that your birthday suggests you are at your best in a supportive team relationship, but when you need autonomy, how do you manage? If you're the boss, are you a good one? Which fields are likely to be the best for your talents? And which the worst? And what about the male/female divide? Is a 9 female boss more desirable than a 9 male colleague?

Here, we get to grips with your career potential, your needs and 'must-have's for job satisfaction, and your loves and loathes work-wise, hopefully highlighting some areas where there is room for you to adjust your manner around others, to help you achieve what it is you're aiming for.

| 9 | 1 | 2 | 3 | 4 | 5 | 6 | 7 | 8 |

In the marketplace

With a thirst for knowledge that reaches into every corner, culture and philosophy, your career talents know no bounds. Your number is akin to the astrological sign Sagittarius, which rules education and knowledge, but, of course, Sagittarius is both an indoors philosopher and an outdoors explorer – and so is a **9** at work.

This says immediately that you need an unconventional set-up, something that gives you freedom to think alongside actual physical space to discover your best gifts. Your direction must be both intellectual and varied, for if you are too tied down to routine you will become plodding and uninspirational – both for yourself and for others. Perhaps this is the reason why so many **9**s find a balance between the security required for financial independence and the opportunity to roam. Taking on several jobs at a time, or working freelance hours, or in a business that presents more than one face to the world, is normal for a **9**.

TEAM PLAYER

Your presence is soothing and uplifting for those around you, so you surely enjoy sociable jobs. Although a **9** can work happily to a deadline or under pressure in isolation, you will probably thrive more when you feel the companionship of working in a cohesive team, and the pleasure of mutually bringing a project to fruition. Working high on intuitive insight, you know when a colleague at the desk down the hall is under siege in their personal life, or chafing against the bad-tempered accountant one floor up. You are the one who brings them a cup of tea and a word of encouragement – and this is a formula for **9**'s success. This almost certainly places you in a position of authority working within a sizeable group, or – if you work in a smaller concern – you may be one person communicating with the wider world. An actor or a writer, for instance, may work in a smaller group, but what they are doing reaches out to many more people once the work goes out into the world.

Because your strength is so often most eloquently expressed in good deeds and kindness to others, the career choices that will be luckiest for you are in areas of counselling and healing, or teaching. This is especially so as you try to finish whatever you start, making you the kind of managerial employee who will give beyond the requisite hours if something is still to be done, or is not yet achieved. It seems **9** has this drive – often to their own detriment – to persevere through the most difficult challenges until all obstacles are overcome.

But sometimes, work-wise, you need to be more pragmatic and cut your losses before you are swallowed by a demanding situation. **9**s so often carry responsibilities and burdens in business, and feel a moral obligation to see things through to the bitterest end. However, you do have the capacity to cope with such stresses – generally, as you also move inexorably towards your desired prize.

WHERE DOES YOUR LIGHT REALLY SHINE?

Here are some of the qualities that **9**s bring to any job:

- The desire to make a better world, and to fight for the underdog, is what may drive you to work in areas like teaching, government office or medicine. You will only be truly fulfilled if you feel your work does make a difference somewhere; **9** is not a number that can be content simply to pick up a pay cheque. Belief in what you are doing is paramount.

- Having mentioned the need for something worthy, it is hardly less important that you find a field of career expression which allows you to unleash your playful and unusual imagination. You have such vision and feeling, and if these aspects of your character and outlook can't sing joyfully in your world of business, you run the risk of becoming one of those negative **9**s who lives in the past, or constantly goes over what might have been.

- Your moods are a well-attested part of your nature, and you need to find work where you can use this change of mood to good effect, rather than to your detriment. This naturally leads to literature, drama and art – creative businesses where different feelings on alternate days can be used positively. Certainly **9** is never static, and you must recognize this when you choose a vocation. You definitely thrive on variety.

- Underneath your considerable creative talents there is a rational and practical mind which allows you to make something useful and something beautiful at the same time. Indeed, **9** possesses a touch of alchemy by understanding how to turn something of negligible value into an object or idea of precious worth. Others will be amazed at your powers of visualization and the creation of an original end product. Any business arena which invites you to use this skill will be just to your taste.

- Movement is a must! Where mortals tire if their work demands regular travel to the point where it is a grind rather than a 'perk', you bring a chintzy-cheerful attitude of away-break to any job that asks you to roam about. And, even if your work sees you commuting on a long train journey every day, your unfettered mind will take the opportunity to invent a concept or design the corner of a new world. Your number literally comes alive when you are on the move.

So, this gives us quite a large canvas to work with. Your happiest situation for work will offer you some free space and changeability, influence with others, and a combination of the creative and the practical. Your talents for inspiration and for good fellow-feeling where others are concerned almost insist that there is a sociable aspect in your work – unlike the ideal for a **1**, a **4** or a **7**, who really prefer quiet time alone. And you should be willing to study and train to grow into your expansive mind, to make the best use of your working gifts.

Let's take a look at a few areas that may hold a particular appeal …

Drama, cinema, TV Your flair for the dramatic cannot be stated too highly, and any work that allows you to use your role-playing skills will see you receive excellent notices. Really, I am of the view that **9**s ought to act or teach acting, or find a related expression of this interest in drama. It is something you are born with and it intrudes even into relationships, where those you are close to aren't quite sure which 'you' will come in today. Thus, work in cinema or film, theatre, opera or dance, and certainly television – which reaches such a vast audience – might be the very best choice for any **9**. And, if this is not the actual nature of your work, how much does the requirement of 'enacting' moods or ideas come into what you must do? Drama is never far from the work of a **9**.

Education This may be the second-best choice – for what other field would allow you this same opportunity of continuing in your own quest for knowledge while inspiring and entertaining other younger minds? Permitted by career choice to read to your heart's content, **9** is the number that rises to the position of control and seniority – the head teacher or dean of the faculty – being both useful and creative. You are a very entertaining lecturer.

Law Working in the legal profession would be another direction suited to the talents just mentioned – particularly as law is another platform for both acting and lecturing. Understanding the power of emotions and the effect of swaying the heart, you can be a good legislator and easily able to mitigate between dissenting parties, even if the courtroom itself is not your chosen domain. But, whatever the field in which you choose to pursue a career, some aspects of the law, or contracts, are likely to fall to a **9**.

Specialist medicine This is another **9** career path, because – like the number **7** – **9** likes to be both the perfectionist and the skilled authority. **7**, though, is more likely to perfect one corner, whereas **9** perfects a wider area – always needing the variety of different tasks to keep you on your toes. But, since **9** rules the hand, the pen and the needle in the creative world, so surgery would be a rewarding vocational platform for a **9** involved in medicine. Other kinds of healing also appeal to you – notably, psychologically complex work soothing the minds of the stressed or the young. A **9** will find the best approach to help someone open up gently, without force.

Recruitment advice/human resources The part of your nature that acts as a 'big brother' figure – in the most positive sense – is suited to working in either vocational guidance or personnel placement. You are so often driven to help others and to encourage them out of malaise, and this makes you the best person to identify what it is that will fulfil them. **9**s are excellent in any aspect of recruitment and career advice, and you always find the time to be both businesslike and sociable with those you help on their way. This may easily extend to training people in this sort of field.

This list isn't exhaustive – a **9**'s talents are invaluable in so many different arenas – but it does offer a taste of what kinds of field will most appeal to your number.

And for luck?

Whatever your work, you will achieve your maximum potential if you use a name to work with that includes the letters I or R. Remember this when you are choosing a company name, if you go into business for yourself. It will help, too, for you to optimize your energy and positive attitude, if you decorate your work environment in the olive/straw hues of very late autumn/early winter. If you are going for an important interview, these colours would make a positive choice in your outfit, as they help you to project yourself in your most powerful and reassuring light.

The 9 female boss

Entering the work space with a **warming smile**, the **9** woman belies her gentle **air of serenity** with a mind that is **keen and focused** on the job at hand. In a world where charm is often a sign of insincerity, the **9** female boss belongs to another reality. Her **charm** is natural and her **concern** for those around her intrinsic, but she is not about to miss an important detail. She is **determined** to finish the job – whatever it may be – to a maximum level of effect, but also to the mutual **enjoyment** of all working with her on it. If it's not fun, she won't be found doing it. At the helm, she can create **fun** for all even in heavy weather conditions.

The **9** boss is **feminine** and beautifully accoutred, but it is not an obsession with her – and such **effortless grace**

9   1   2   3   4   5   6   7   8

lifts the morale of her team or the clients she works with. Not that everyone likes her, oddly enough: some people find her almost too good to be true, and look for the trick, not wanting to be caught out. Perhaps the **9** female who has risen to the top exposes the selfishness in others' behaviour to their own discomfort, but she is unlikely to confront them herself in any ill-mannered way. She seems to achieve **harmony** in the workplace by osmosis, and over time she will attract the perfect colleagues to help her make an **altruistic business** that brings a fair return, with room to include arts and travel as part of her daily working landscape. This is clever, if you think about it.

She might be the senior consultant who still makes time to listen to her patients' fears with a **generous** bed-side manner; or the theatre director who has vast respon-sibility but takes time to foster an encouraging bond with the youngest member of the company; or the head teacher who **cares** if her staff are overworked, and is more

8 7 6 5 4 3 2 1 9

than willing to take as many classes herself as she can fit in. Perhaps she is the senior researcher who can stay emotionally involved in a story yet bring it with stark clarity to a reader; or she is the seasoned diplomat who hasn't given up **hope** of good human relations in deference to bureaucracy. She is a **mystery**, loving **variety**, preferring classic Chanel perfume one day and a modern green-tea fragrance the next; but she is also **analytical**, and a woman of **substance**. Don't nap on the job with a **9** woman in charge!

WORK PROFILE
The 9 male boss

Beneath the **cheeky** grin that says he is just **one of the boys**, the **9** male boss is an excellent captain for the ship, because he has a **vision** for where life could be headed. He is **clever** and well-read, but he wears his knowledge lightly and rarely chooses to expose others' ignorance for the sake of asserting control. His style is to be more **pragmatic**, carefully correcting false notions and subtly but **authoritatively** offering an alternative view – which is, of course, the best one on which to proceed. He is **sympathetic** to other people's misfortunes and worries, but he is no pushover, **determined** to make a streamlined workforce which gets results while maintaining a sunny work atmosphere at the same time.

Sounds too good to be true? Well, his personal life

8 7 6 5 4 3 2 1 **9**

reflects the difficulty of finding a modus operandi when there is such strong **conflict** between his emotions and his common sense, and he is always **struggling** to find control in his family life because he gives a little too much of himself to the rest of the world. But most people will forgive him: his **humour** is a joy, and his boyish good looks – which last well into advanced age – have a **compelling** quality that invites others to agree to very nearly anything he asks of them. This is something that's worth remembering if you are one of the colleagues giving up another weekend to **do his bidding**! Yet his work team will agree to do this, time and time again. The **9** male boss gives more than just what's on the page – and he expects others to do so also.

He is **affectionate** and **generous** with his staff and peers, and will remember birthdays – or at least have a system in place to help him do so. And, if things do go wrong, he will be determined to set them right himself, never passing the buck but always ready to **accept his own culpability**. In short, the **9** male boss is more of a **big brother** to a family of working friends than an efficient despot. But, he does get results.

8   7   6   5   4   3   2   1   9

WORK PROFILE
The 9 female employee

It must be *possible* to have a **9** female employee, but she seems to be working for herself, **in her own way**, at her own pace, from the day she arrives. She is **willing** to please everyone, and yet there is nothing fawning in her behaviour. If she doesn't like something she will say so, but usually not in a very confrontational way. She can be a little **secretive** – which adds to the **air of mystery** about her – and her co-workers will wonder whether she is spending her lunch-hour at a quick yoga class, or browsing the nearest good bookshop. Both are equally likely. She may even be **reserved** and seem a touch proud, until everyone gets to know her better.

She is quite **private**, and yet also very **public** and **kind** to people. This **paradox** is at the root of **9**'s nature, and

| 9 | 1 | 2 | 3 | 4 | 5 | 6 | 7 | 8 |

it will come out nowhere as strongly as in the **9** female employee, because she is watching, learning, **listening intently**, ready to speak when there is something **intelligent** that needs to be said, but also **ready to observe** when someone she respects has the floor. Her first few months may see her overwork purely in the attempt to come to grips with what she has been thrust into. She is not a sycophant.

Who she sees in her personal life may be a subject for discussion: she likes **variety**, even though she can be very **loyal**, and she may have dated (or be dating) a rock star or a painter and decorator – snobbishness never coming into it. She is **witty**, and her education may contain a few surprises. No one can sum her up until she has been there for a while ...

... By which time, in my view, she is likely to be less of the employee and more of the girl **on her way up** – a sub-manager or form mistress, the youngest person to be seconded to the executive floor in years, perhaps. She gets there through her **patient goodwill** and willingness to learn what she doesn't know, but she's a **smart cookie** and understands what is required. She is **prepared** for a dozen possibilities – her handbag ever ready to produce the emergency nail file or needle and thread. 'Employee' is a short-term post for this interesting young **9** woman!

WORK PROFILE
The 9 male employee

He has a nice sense of **humour**, and no one can believe he is as old as he says he is. There is a **grinning warmth** about him which doesn't quite cover his **perceptive** mind and clever ideas. He is a **jack of all trades** – annoying for the specialists who have been there longer than him but know little more of their subject than he does, while he can go on into other realms of professionalism. He is **proficient** at IT, knows his way around research, has a good head for figures, and – if the boss is busy – he can address the clients with **flair** and humour while covering every salient point. He is quite a successful **entertainment committee** all in one package.

He may desire to be a **peaceful** soul and keep clear of office politics, but if he is asked for an opinion he can

8   7   6   5   4   3   2   1   9

be both honest and **diplomatic**. His **eloquence** sets him a little apart from others in the team, and he is able to **persuade** many people to try their hand at something they feel initially reluctant to do. This may be true of the boys bonding in the great outdoors, or the squash game, or the new Japanese restaurant which he can describe with such energy that even the vegetarians will give it a go! He is **hard to deny**.

In the boardroom he gets the results he wants personally through a **subtle** approach, and he looks cool and comfortable in an open-necked shirt under a well-cut suit, even when others feel compelled to find a tie. He has his own **style** and character in pretty much everything, to which no one really takes offence.

All will be well, as long as he leaves his emotions at the door – for this is the only thing likely to disturb the **9** male employee's route to the top. The ladies who work around him are either inclined to mother him or see if they can get him to talk – which is never so hard, if the one offering the ear is kind and intelligent. He is **seducible**, because he can be **restless**. Perhaps this is one of the things he needs to overcome for the sake of his happy heart and fulfilment of his working hopes. But he is a **pleasure** to have on any workforce – good company, **bright** and **dedicated**. If he is using his wit to outdo others, he is the rare bad apple in the barrel. Mostly, the **9** male employee is just the person one would hire for any post that demands **versatility**.

Ideal world or cruel world?
Best and worst jobs ...

IN AN IDEAL WORLD

Best job for a 9 female: Director of an arts firm such as a gallery or museum (demands her skills to address the public at regular gatherings and throw parties to charitable purpose, clairvoyant skills also helpful)

Best job for a 9 male: Theatre impresario or film company chief executive (can make decisions about funding projects that have content as well as box-office appeal, intuition put to the test)

IN A CRUEL WORLD

Worst job for a 9 female: Manager of a charity shop (will feel the wish to give away designer clothes to anyone who needs them regardless of store policy, too 'small-time' for her liking)

Worst job for a 9 male: Juggler in a circus (allows for travel, but has no room for expansion; if he were the circus manager, all would be well!)

9'S CHILDHOOD

Seeing the way a number expresses itself in someone very young is fascinating, for the tendencies and responses are all in their infancy – and yet plain to see. Some facets of a number's power need to be grown into, and take time to reveal how they will be dealt with by the developing character. Sometimes the strength of a number can be a frustration when we're young.

If looking back on your own childhood through the lens of your number, you should discover – with considerable humour and irony – a renewed understanding of some of the difficulties or excitements you experienced. Or, if you have a child who is also a **9**, you may learn something more useful; it is an advantage to understand the qualities a

| 8 | 7 | 6 | 5 | 4 | 3 | 2 | 1 | 9 |

number exudes over an awakening personality, especially in relation to talents and career strengths, as it might save a lot of frustrations. You'll be able to appreciate the positive traits, and handle negative ones more sympathetically.

Here, we take a detailed look at what it's like to be a child bearing your number. But what about the other numbers? Perhaps you have a child who is a **3**, and you'd like to know what that means? Or maybe you'd like to gain insight into friends' and siblings' childhoods, to see if it sheds any light on the people they have become today? A short profile is given for each number, along with advice for a **9** parent on dealing with other-number offspring.

Just as your own parents would have discovered when you were a child, the challenge with a **9** child is in helping them to cope with that heightened potential to understand the needs and feelings of others, and to embrace their philanthropic sense of responsibility without denying the fulfilment of individual need. It's a balancing act ...

9   1   2   3   4   5   6   7   8

The young 9

The young **9** arrived in the family's life to bring a touch of humanity and goodness – to be, in various ways, beautiful and kind to all. Musical, artistic, romantic and vivid in all senses, the **9** child is born for the theatre and the arts, wanting to travel the world and befriend everyone.

9 children have an expansive view of things even in their youthful understanding, and they don't like to be restricted. But they are serious, and, even if they have a characteristic dryish humour with warmth of personality, they will still project a sincerity – and even an intensity – about their young lives. They listen to others very carefully and evaluate what they say with lively interest. They can often feel let down by discovering that others rarely live up to their idealized impressions of them – and this hurts. A **9** child will always prefer to see the good in someone if

8   7   6   5   4   3   2   1   9

possible, but when a friend or authority figure speaks without kind feeling, or to deliberately hurt another, the young **9** is harshly disillusioned.

Understanding what is personal and what is impersonal becomes a major growth point for a **9**, and sometimes a confusion about which is which will make this developing person seem inconsistent. At one moment they are kind and generous, and at another they are more distanced and cool, more self-interested. It takes a few years for a **9** to assume their tremendous spiritual and humanitarian potential and yet survive in a real and flawed world.

With a good head for both science and the arts, there are many career directions a **9** child may wish to take, so a parent will have their work cut out trying to help them choose. However, because the number **9** is like a mirror, these children are able to take on the feelings of just about anyone, which is why they are so artistic and good at drama and writing. If you're a **9** parent of a **9** child,

9's toys

Pets (very important for a 9) • Toy theatre • Dressing-up box • Video camera • Music systems and instruments – especially to play in groups (e.g. strings) • Chess set • Backgammon • Quality paints • Telescope • Books and more books • Personalized small luggage

you will remember the hilarity you caused by mimicking the teacher or repeating the words of others with a little extra caricature, and you will also recall the pleasure of being so entertaining.

From their first years in school it will be clear a **9** child has a lovely dry sense of humour and a taste for the unusual. They are not often prejudiced and seem to be easy-going – although they are sensitive to the atmosphere around them, picking up the vibes like a sponge. If you speak to them harshly they will take it seriously, and they are protective of others who seem to be hurt in this way, too. A **9** child's mission is to cheer others, and to make vivid and real what is most beautiful, not what is necessarily sad. This takes its toll, of course, in many ways: the young **9** is frequently thinking of what the other person needs to hear, rather than what they may wish to get off their own chest.

Though a **9** can be selfish, it is the selfishness of wanting others to be the way they *wish* them to be – and of being self-obsessed when someone shatters their illusion. They may express this distress mildly, but be sure that a **9** child feels it acutely. It is the first step to acquiring wisdom, and to becoming a shade more realistic about the world they live in and the necessary, slower steps it may take to make changes. But they will always be trying to change what they don't like.

Perhaps the most significant thing about a **9** child is their delicate relationship with their parents – but particularly with that all-important father figure. The father's/father figure's influence can be the cause of the greatest happiness to a **9** child – or the greatest regret. A **9** girl will want to idolize her dad, and will feel desperately disappointed if circumstances are against this; and a **9** boy may wish to emulate his father – and yet they often grow up without enough input from this important person because he is busy or away. It seems a **9** child must be wise ahead of their time, and so this lesson is thrown at them in one guise or another.

The 1 child

This resourceful child has a different way of thinking, and will stand to one side and evaluate things without pressure. Repeat Grandma's sound advice on any subject to a **1** under the age of six, and they'll simply ask, 'Why?' Ignoring the social expectation to conform, **1** children often make us laugh with surprise.

A **1** child is tough and active – an inquisitive soul who wants to get on with things and not be held in check by others, however wise the parental eye might be. Stubborn and impatient, **1**s frequently suffer by questioning – though not from rudeness – the authority of a parent or teacher. **1**s break down tradition and find new ideas to form a fresh understanding of the world we're in. Your **1** child needs careful handling: a bright mind bursting with interest and disinclined to authority needs subtle direction. If **1** children dominate their friends and talk over their family it can make them socially inept and unable to co-operate in love relationships later in life, leading to loneliness rather than just self-reliance.

A **1**'s greatest challenge is to learn to live in a social world and understand that they are not inevitably right. To foster a **1**'s unique personality and avoid insensitivity to others, let them behave like an adult. This confidence a **1** child will ably repay. **1** children suffer from being misunderstood, as they're often so happy in their private hours and so demanding of having their own time that they may not learn to express their need for others. The seeds are sown early as to how to approach another person for signs of affection, and a wise **9** parent may wish to 'invade' their **1** child's space, offering comfort and good counsel regularly. Sometimes you must hold back a fraction, and let them signal their need — albeit subtly; otherwise, your independent **1** could simply break free.

8　7　6　5　4　3　2　1　9

The 2 child

All children born on the 2nd or 20th need affection and a peaceful environment to grow up in. Those born on the 11th or 29th are a little different, being master number **11**s with **2** as the denominator, and they have an old head on young shoulders from the start. But even they – for all their drive toward excitement and adventure – will be happiest if their home life is mostly secure and tranquil.

These highly sensitive and intuitive children know what you will say before you say it. They are also dreamy and process ideas in their sleep, waking to instinctive and wise solutions to their problems. But they are vulnerable, and need reassuring more than most numbers. They are acutely sensitive to criticism, feeling that all comments are proof that they're not quite good enough, so you need to deliver your words with tact and an awareness of their needs.

9	1	2	3	4	5	6	7	8

2 children are talented artists, actors, dancers and/or musicians: they know how others *feel*. A **2** child prefers to support friends and family as often as possible, and this can make them a doormat ready to be walked on unless those they live with are alert to their inclinations. If the **2** is an **11**, the wish to help out will be very strong indeed, but these children also have a finely tuned moral sense and will be offended by injustice – especially against them! Don't dish out judgement until you have all the facts.

2s are good healers and can make others feel better – even from their earliest years. Knowing when to cuddle or touch and when to be quiet, they often have a stillness that works miracles around the sick, the sad and the elderly. A **9** parent will respect this, always ready with praise, appreciating their **2** child's need for harmony, as well as their kindness. They have a similar feeling for what's right and wrong, and for the needs of others, and you will enjoy the affection and support you receive from your intelligent **2**.

| 8 | 7 | 6 | 5 | 4 | 3 | 2 | 1 | 9 |

The 3 child

From the cradle, **3**s hold parties and like to mix with other children. They have a capacity to laugh and precipitate laughter, even when things go a little wrong. **3** children are like the reappearing sun after rain, and their energies can be restorative for everyone. Creative and playful, nothing keeps them low for long.

Like a juggler keeping plates and balls in the air, **3**s have several activities and talents on the go from the start. This can be a problem, however: making decisions is hard for them, and they need a wise older counsellor who can talk out the options and give them room to think. Even then, a decision once reached can always be changed – and a **3** child will find a way to run in several directions at one time.

Keep your **3** busy with lots of artistic activities, using colours and textures – right from babyhood – to open their eyes to what they can do. Even before the age of ten a strong personal taste will begin to develop – and it may not be the same as their parents'. Using up their flow of energy on a multitude of tasks will be demanding on both parents, but the **3** child does give a great deal back in return.

3s are talkers and have a witty repartee, even when tiny: you'll be surprised at what you hear from them sometimes, and will wonder where it came from. Naturally gifted at PR, they will talk you around when you are set against one of their wishes, but you will need to direct them now and again or nothing will ever be finished! A **9** parent with a **3** child will give them freedom to experiment, and won't try to control them too much or be irritated if they are disorganized, or chatter wildly. Wise and kind, you won't worry if they rush about without your directed purpose; they have a way of coming back smiling.

| 8 | 7 | 6 | 5 | 4 | 3 | 2 | 1 | 9 |

The 4 child

Surprisingly insecure and in need of praise, these children are reliable and hard-working and want to do well. They are their own worst critics at times, and they glow when appreciated. They are happiest with family around them – even extended members – and often prefer holidays in familiar places. That said, they can be very quiet and self-sufficient when required, for they concentrate well.

These are organized children who won't cope well if their parents aren't as organized as they are! Never lose a school form or an item from their games kit on a crucial day, as this will cause them serious panic. They like to have material possessions around them because this bolsters their feeling of security, and will manage their pocket money well, content to do odd jobs and chores to gain this reward.

4s love the earth and buildings. They will treasure a

patch of garden given them to tend, or a garden house they can extend or build outright. If they are born on the 22nd, rather than the 4th, 13th or 31st, they will truly have architectural talents, and may follow design as a career later. All **4** children, though, are handy at craft work and excellent at projects which require intelligence combined with method to get something done. They hate being late and don't admire tardiness in others, either.

As children, **4**s are loyal and dependable to family and friends, and are more patient than many numbers. They will make light of complex tasks, but they need to be allowed to do things in their own way. A **9** parent will be amazed at the care and order their **4** child takes, but perhaps think them slightly self-interested or unimaginative. They simply have a different approach to life. **4**s feel responsible to others, though, which you'll encourage. Your patient direction and their good focus blend well, and you will admire their tenacity. The relationship will grow closer with time.

8   7   6   5   4   3   2   1   9

The 5 child

Unable to be confined or sit still, a **5** child is bursting with curiosity. Very sociable and happy to be on the move, these adventurous youngsters have much in common with **1s**, but are more willing to work in a team, and good at picking up on other people's ideas, only to improve them.

From their first few words, **5** children have good memories and a facility for speech – they speak and learn quickly, and can pick up more than one language. Even more physical than **1s** (although the two numbers are alike in this), they are excellent at sport or physical co-ordination. They chatter, are full of energy, and like to play to an audience. But most importantly, **5** children love to be free – to explore, laze, hunt, create, discover and travel. Take your **5** child away on holiday and they quickly make friends with others, and acquire a taste for foreign places. They will even experiment with different food, if you're lucky.

5s find a reason to slip away if they're bored with adult company — so don't be offended. Their minds can pursue several streams of active interest, so they need a great deal of amusement to stretch them. This adventurous spirit can be a worry to their family sometimes and, indeed, **5**s need to understand house rules about asking first, or telling someone where they're off to. The difficulty is that **5** children usually don't want to explain themselves to anyone.

The test for a **5**'s parent is to set their child constructive challenges that will vent their curiosity in good ways. **5**s will pick up technology and music (other forms of language, in a sense) quickly, but they don't like dull routine work — which will irritate a **4** sibling if they have one. A **9** parent of a **5** child will offer them freedom to do their own thing, but will be tested by their constant restlessness and noise; nevertheless, you'll admire their imaginative talent and creativity. Be patient, though!

The 6 child

Here's a young soul in need of a peaceful haven, just like a **2**, but a **6** will literally feel ill if there is dissension around them. Always wanting to beautify their surroundings and make pretty presents for Mum, these talented, sensitive children have many gifts for creative expression. They will also nurse the sick cat or anyone who needs gentle kindness, but are not always robust themselves, and should be sheltered from bad weather or aggressive viruses.

As children, **6**'s musical talents should emerge – and they often have beautiful speaking or singing voices. They are also the peacemakers of the family – natural creators of balance and harmony. Give them a free hand with their bedroom and their flower garden, and be ready to learn from them. Both boys and girls usually make good cooks when they are older, too, so time spent in the kitchen won't be wasted. Birthday presents that foster their good eye — a camera or set of art tools — will usually fit them well.

Despite being sensitive to others and quite intuitive, **6** as a child is a little shy and needs drawing out — especially if there has been much change in their young life, because **6** children need stability and like to remain a tiny bit traditional. They become very attached to their home. But if their family life is unconventional they will ultimately adjust, because they offer their family a lot of love, and like to be shown love in return. Even the boys have a feminine side which in no way calls their gender into question.

Good at school and almost as well-organized as **4**s, this is a number which needs time to grow into itself: **6**s are enormously talented. A **9** parent will see this, and be kind and appreciative towards their artistic, sensitive **6** child. And when you need a friend to listen, support, encourage and back *you* up, you will find unsuspected reservoirs of strength in this interesting child.

The 7 child

This is a child with a focused mind and a strongly developed critical sense. A **7** child is perceptive and, sometimes, disarmingly quiet. They will often prefer adult company, as their peers will probably seem too young and underdeveloped to them. Wise and difficult to know well, these are children with a serious cast to their intelligent minds.

The fact that a **7** child can sit quietly and contemplate things deeply should not imply that they are introverted: quite the opposite. A **7** will grow into a very good host as long as the company appeals, and they have a lovely sense of humour, apparent from their earliest years – even if it does sometimes find expression at others' expense. They will rarely be rude, but certainly have a good understanding of all that has been said – and what has not been. Listen to their impressions of the people they deal with!

| 9 | 1 | 2 | 3 | 4 | 5 | 6 | 7 | 8 |

All **7**s as children have an inward reluctance to accept other people's ideas automatically, but there is a special propensity to independence in a child born on the 16th. This is the number of someone who finds it difficult asking for what they want – someone who often feels as though they haven't been consulted as to their own wishes. And all **7**s certainly have definite ideas about what to believe.

7 children should be told the truth on virtually all matters; they will know if they are being deceived, and will respect being treated as an adult in any case – which an equally truthful **9** parent always prefers to do. Perhaps only you won't find their maturity a little unnerving, and you will respect your **7** child's inner strength and drive to excel in what they like. Though different – a **7** child wanting to retire more into privacy and personal space than friendly **9** – your numbers appreciate each other, and a **7** child gives any parent much to be proud of, both academically and in terms of humanitarian feelings.

The 8 child

Here we have a young executive in the making. Even when they are still at school these children have a canny nose for what will make good business – and yet they are generous, hard-working and prepared to learn everything it will take to succeed in this life. Children born on the 8th, 17th and 26th like to have charge of their own finances, and to be given scope to do 'grown-up' activities – organizing their own parties and making arrangements for outings with their friends.

These children have strength and energy, but mentally are reflective and wise, too. They always see both sides to an argument – so parents who ask them to choose sides, beware! An **8** makes good judgements, and even before the age of ten they have a sense of what is fair and what is morally right.

| 9 | 1 | 2 | 3 | 4 | 5 | 6 | 7 | 8 |

As this number rules the octave, many **8** children are extremely musical and have a wonderful sense of rhythm. This last even assures they can be good at sport, as it takes innate timing to perfect many physical skills. **8**s also like philosophical ideas and relish being given 'big concepts' to chew over, especially concerning politics or religious ideas. **8**s are proud, and like to research things carefully – so as long as they are not bored, you will find an **8** child with their head in a book or on the internet, or watching programmes that educate and broaden their vistas.

An **8** child is always striving for balance, like you, though you must be pragmatic if they sometimes pull in the opposite direction. Though independent, they are loyal to those they love, and a delicate sensibility makes them look at the other side of a story, or fight for an underdog. You understand this feeling for others very well, and mostly you will respect the qualities and mind of your **8** child, who is generous, driven and philosophical, just as you are.

8 7 6 5 4 3 2 1 9

9 AT PLAY

We have discovered how your number expresses itself through your character in relation to your family and your general personality, what instinctive reactions go with your number in everyday situations, and how it might shape your career path and colour your childhood. But every day our DAY number also influences the way we respond to the social world around us. So, what can it say about our leisure hours? Is yours a number that even allows itself to relax? (Well, you probably already have some answers to this one!) What can your number reveal about the way you like to spend your time, or how you achieve pleasure outside of duty?

9   1   2   3   4   5   6   7   8

Over the next few pages we take a look at what makes you tick, as a **9**, when you are unwinding – and how **9**s prefer to fill their time, if given a choice. Let's see whether you're typical in this respect ... And who knows – if you haven't already tried all the activities and pastimes mentioned, maybe you'll get a few ideas about what to put on your list for next time!

The 9 woman at play

The vital part of a **9**'s character is the empathy you have for the sorrows of the world and the hurts of friends and family; yet a **9** girl knows how to have fun, too! Never all tremulous feeling without humour, you get your party shoes on and go out on the ice – with or without blades. Being a creature of mood and the heat of the moment, the **9** woman entices others to try things they've never tried, and go where they've never been. In your leisure time, life is to be explored!

Travel must be the first point of reference for a **9** with time on her hands. Like **5**, restlessness gets into your bones, and at the first whiff of an invitation to pack a bag you'll be shopping for hiking boots, or snow-shoes, or diving equipment. Though **9** is not an especially sporty number, it is physical and an adventurer, so you will quickly prepare to

9   1   2   3   4   5   6   7   8

tame a fear of anything unknown. A weekend off doesn't have to span three days to provide a window for a walk in the mountains or a flight to a foreign city for a change of gear. Charter flights that offer city breaks and last-minute weekend treats are bookmarked on a **9** lady's laptop. You know where to browse for late get-away deals, and your luggage is hardly pristine after a twelve-month period!

Back at home, you are a sensitive and diverting companion. You love having friends around, and – even if you're often away for work – your domestic space has an air of tranquillity or restfulness which makes a perfect spa retreat for a girlfriend with heartache. A **9** lady will pledge many a day off to provide tapas and tissues for a friend in need. And, once the clarion call goes out, the table may extend to many newcomers arriving for a little piece of your wise mind. You're used to it, and such evenings given over to others somehow form part of your own leisure, along with paintbrushes and concert tickets. But you will hope for a return of the favour when you need to open your heart, too. And, with so many friends from so many places, all with different cultural viewpoints to offer, you are spoiled for choice about where to mend a bruised heart.

If you have found your rhythm in life and have a happy romance, you may simply declare that Monday night is 'Girls' Cinema Night' – a favourite – or that Sunday brunch is the perfect time for discussing books or reading plays with a like-minded group. Not to make you sound too highbrow, you need stimulus, and love burying your head in any cover or title that catches your interest (have a look at the size of a **9**'s bookshelves; only an **8** may boast a greater number of volumes, though they won't necessarily have read them all!). The **9** girl is sure to be the one who takes over everyone's travel arrangements, or purchase of cinema tickets, or choice-of-restaurant-after booking. It is different in mood every time.

If you are working all weekend, your leisure can be

squeezed into the tea break, when you select a bag from the half-dozen different flavours you have as normal fare. Add one slice of something simple, and you have converted ten stolen minutes into a satisfying head-trip and battery recharge. A **9** woman's sense of leisure and pleasure is in her mind.

But the most perfect free time of all will be spent with the one you love. Although **7** is more selective about the friends they choose than **9**, **9** is *extremely* selective about the one they love; and your happy hour is too short unless there is a vision of romance that comes into it. Time given to girlfriends and work pals is generously donated, but you're a romantic who loves spending time with her lover. This is icing on the cake, and the cake can be picnic-packed and eaten anywhere. At sunrise on a ferry or at midnight on a beach, **9** girls come out to play when passion stirs them. You are most relaxed and joyful when leisure is about love.

| 8 | 7 | 6 | 5 | 4 | 3 | 2 | 1 | 9 |

The 9 man at play

Sacrificing some of his own wishes in the interests of the people he loves, the **9** man with free time includes others in his plans. You are generous and kindly, but you do get your little moods as well, so it will behove those who love you to stretch out halfway and meet your needs.

You want to give, want others to be on your emotional map, and prefer to fill up your hours with activity and thought rather than idle time-wasting. Like your female counterpart, your urge to travel is strong, and your wish will be to take the world and their brother along with you: budget willing, **9** men are the ones who book the villa in Tuscany or up by the lakes big enough for all to join. You think of what will please the people you care about — and there are a lot of them!

Being a keen reader and a good thinker, you fill your

holiday time – in any location – with beach reads and museum visits, and are culturally aware of the sensitive feelings of the people who live there. You wouldn't dream of dropping into a foreign country without a few courteous words in the native tongue, so you probably have a smattering of every language from Zulu and Hindi to Tunisian Arabic. You only regret it's not enough for a whole intellectual conversation – but you can work out a lot from the faces of everyone you meet.

You have an eye for photography (honed on so many trips) and a way with cooking, and you like learning more in your leisure time. **9** men are happy to be self-taught: education is not the way you prefer to fill your hours, unless you feel strongly that you've missed out in your earlier life. You love digesting information through your senses – the reading and the listening being only slightly more effective than the talent you have for understanding just by feeling what it is like to be in someone else's shoes.

And you like slipping on many different pairs for a taste of what another life may be like. The **9** man may go hunting, shooting and fishing (though you may not be too keen to kill anything!), and can negotiate skis or French bicycles at will. Others should always remember, though, that you have moods, and they all need to be appeased.

To entertain your intellectual energies, books and films probably dominate your conscious mind – but music is vital, too. You are an arts man, with a practical head and a taste for mystery and the esoteric – which is quite some diversity, by most people's standards. You can sit comfortably in a yoga class if asked, and are willing to learn to do some needlework if there is a reason for it. **9** men are usually in touch with their feminine side, so there is little concern with regard to hobbies that may be thought of as traditionally gender-divided.

The only thing your close loved ones need to understand is that you have to have some private time to think about the best way to handle your life and responsibilities – and you have to have public time as part of your friendly nature. You are personal and impersonal in all your responses to life. Your free time will echo that, and others who share it must be flexible.

9 IN LOVE

Love: it's what we all want to know about. What's your style as a lover? And your taste – where does that run? Do you want a partner who is, ideally, as good at mixing and as gregarious as you? Or would you be more at ease with a lover who takes their cue from you, enjoying learning with you and quietly following behind at their own pace? Everything you do is about exploration and discovery, but is this equally applicable to your love life?

Our first task is to consider how you see others as potential partners, and what you are likely to need from them. Why are you attracted to someone in the first place? This is where we begin ... But then you might like to pass the book across to your other half (if you have one), for the second subject of discussion is: why are *they* attracted to *you*? What does it mean to have a **9** lover?

Telltale traits of the 9 lover

- Very romantic
- A little idealistic
- Definite wishes in love and strong urge to make them happen
- Inclined to brood over losses, but this is reworked into wisdom for the next relationship
- Sometimes secretive about or towards a lover
- Has both a sunny side and dark side (at times) in love affairs

---

How do you do?
A 9 IN ATTRACTION

Always ahead of the crowd – or perhaps, more truly, unconcerned whether they agree with your taste – **9**s are drawn to the most interesting and mysterious person in a room. With your affable and approachable manner, and your distinctive style which emits sparkle and warmth in the most serene wrapping, you are a lighthouse for others to come and talk to at any gathering or grouping ... but the person you want is the one who hangs back on you. Smoothly chatting to the colourful cast of characters who have sought you out, you juggle your own witticisms and interest in the person who is openly agreeing with your sharp criticism of the film or play you just saw, with a subtly roving eye which picks out that fascinating soul quietly holding court with a group of admirers in the far corner.

| 9 | 1 | 2 | 3 | 4 | 5 | 6 | 7 | 8 |

It's not that a **9** is attracted to the one they can't have — that is for others — but **9** is magnetically pulled towards the most interesting and unusual person at any gathering. They may be beautiful, but never obvious. **9** insists on looking below the surface.

A **9** will be attracted to someone with looks, humour and an educated mind, each of which is an essential quality if your passion and mind are to be fired. But this can mean that you are courting a love who expects to be admired and the centre of everyone's attention — someone who is used to having a lot of choice. This is the very lover you can be lured to build up illusions over, and because **9**s can be so affectionate and loyal you become desperately stung when you discover that the object of your affection isn't flawless, but probably has a past or a current second string of romantic interest that will captivate a number of hearts.

You despair when the one you love proves faithless in

any way, but for some reason, **9** must go through these impossible tests. You cannot fall for a mortal being, and are more likely to love someone who has been hurt and needs you, but who is deep and clever and a magnet for trouble. A **9** falls in love where they are least likely to have an easy path to joy. So why do you keep doing this? Because, as you well know, you want to grow and feel for other people, and sometimes this is a masochistic tendency.

A lasting relationship will come, though, when you achieve some personal balance. The talent to live life to the full, and to exude an easy but sincere charm, is with you from your early days, but what confuses those you would love is that at times you seem to be cold and distant, judgemental and impossible to please, while at other times you couldn't be more funny, tolerant and easygoing. Or perhaps you confuse your lover by seeming to be totally unrealistic, caught up with dreams that no other person can believe will come to be. No doubt this is largely a matter of your moodiness, and if it can't be controlled it can lead you to unnecessary losses and emotional sorrow.

Vive la différence!

You look for beauty of character almost so more than what is skin-deep — and when you fall in love with that extraordinary person who embodies your idea of perfection, you will fall with intensity. **9**'s emotions are not mild, but even when you love, you may hanker for something from your past or for someone who connects with another part of your soul. **9** isn't fickle, but you are attracted to variety — different qualities — and it is unusual to find all this in any single individual. It may be that the one you love will need to accept that other people fill a separate role in your life — a hybrid role of being friend and love, though not lover. Your number finds many platonic soulmates — people with whom you share a secret part of your

8   7   6   5   4   3   2   1   9

being without necessarily posing a threat to your central love relationship. So, it becomes clear that the love you are drawn to must do more than just tolerate this need in you. If you give your affection to someone who proves to be jealous or possessive, the romance may quickly fade.

So what do you want from this ideal lover? Simply, a person with beauty of soul and form, who can be constructively busy while you are dreaming and losing all track of time, and who has a sense of humour to match your own, and a mind prepared for much philosophical speculation and discussion. It is inconceivable that you can give your heart to someone who is shallow or just a pretty face: **9**s are one of the two or three numbers who most strongly seek a soulmate. If someone is petty or behaves without grace, they will badly let you down. And you may find that the love who really turns you upside down is, well, a little strange to others' minds. Not a particularly tall order to find, then?

To have and to hold?

LOVING A NUMBER 9

We all know why you have fallen for this huggable, kind-hearted soul who makes time for everyone's sob story. Sexy, ever-youthful **9** is popular with everyone, of both sexes, and there's a queue even to get close enough to talk to them – never mind do any flirting. Perhaps it is that fascinating truth that this attractive human being knows so many unconventional people? It is a tantalizing character trait that, in every street, or even in different countries, you can stroll along listening to a gentle bubble of intelligent conversation from your **9** when someone shouts 'Hello!' or invites you to join them at the table for a bite. Long-lost friends of a **9** are everywhere to be found; and what an inviting mystery!

After that smile and facility to change voice and facial

shape like a true mimic cajoled you into laughter, you may have been charmed by your **9**'s generosity, or their astonishingly well-informed mind. Even on the third or fourth date – when initial impressions are normally collapsing into not-unpleasant reality with most romantic attractions – **9** is still wrong-footing you with their grasp of so many various subjects.

Like the languages they can roll off their tongue with conviction, if not perfect command, your magnetic **9** can converse with you about the books you have both read, the places you both like, the political situations in the most far-flung places that they know about, too. This is a little disconcerting, for these may be your mastermind subjects, and you wonder how anyone can casually almost match you in such a string of interests. And, of course, there's plenty more where that came from.

| 9 | 1 | 2 | 3 | 4 | 5 | 6 | 7 | 8 |

Share and share alike

The up side of falling for a **9** is that life will never be predictable or banal. A romantic weekend away could turn into anything from an impromptu film shoot to a cookery class in southern France, or to a hop-picking expedition in a sunny corner of the countryside with lazy lanes and a wonderful scent – because *this* person you have alighted on is romantic, and will surprise you over and again. But heed the advice not to include your best friends in the trip, because they'll monopolize your love with questions about everything from badly trained pets and children to difficult mothers-in-law and feisty bosses. **9** seems to have an answer to it all – but it can get in the way when you just want to cuddle up and get closer. Or, it might be that weighty paperback that absorbs your **9**'s attention more than you do – at least for a few hours. Loving a **9** is about sharing, and doing things their way. Though, in fairness, it must be said that your grown-up **9** will forgive you if you over-react to an imagined slight, or when you let loose about the stressful day you've had. **9** has seen it all before, and knows how to smooth these wrinkles from your brow.

It is thrilling to see your charming **9** – with youthful good looks – take over a dull party and inject some life into it. One of the reasons you love them is that they have the gift of the gab and an attentive ear, all at the same time. Your **9** lover can carry off an ethnic look or appear resplendent in head-to-toe couture depending on mood and occasion, and being at home with either the 'Bohemian artist' set or the 'heads of state' is very alluring. There is never an end to the surprises and the pleasures that come with dating a **9** – not to mention that they're sensual and romantic in the bedroom, caring, giving and very tactile. So, surely we have just described a creature of perfection?

9 **1** **2** **3** **4** **5** **6** **7** **8**

The problems that come with loving a **9** may not be obvious for a while, and when they arise they seem a shock. This wonderful person has a knack for sabotaging their own happiness, worrying that all good things can so easily come to an end, and feeling that the pattern of previous heartbreaks must be a source of future pain, too. And then they may retreat a little not to get hurt, or become cooler and more chillingly rational, and all that romantic fun is gone.

How to cope? Ride out the moods, if you love your **9**, and don't go into this half-heartedly. Your **9** is entertaining, but more than a role-player. A deep human being lives behind the sunny wrapping, and it takes a grown-up, patient person to open them up. Do so gently – and prepare for something special.

9 in love

Turn-ons:
- ♥ ✔ Someone to share a dream with
- ♥ ✔ A person willing to broaden their view and enter an event or situation with an open mind
- ♥ ✔ A lover with humour and resilience who is not easily made jealous
- ♥ ✔ Somone willing to travel!

Turn-offs:
- ♥ ✘ A lover who wants assurances of the future
- ♥ ✘ Someone who takes control of your address book and film collection
- ♥ ✘ Anyone lacking in conversation and knowledge
- ♥ ✘ A person without substance (no matter how gorgeous they may be!)

9'S COMPATIBILITY

In this weighty section you have the tools to find out how well you click with all the other numbers in matters of the heart, but also when you have to work or play together too. Each category opens with a star-ratings chart, showing you – at a glance – whether you're going to encounter plain sailing or stormy waters in any given relationship. First up is love: if your number matches up especially well with the person you're with, you will appreciate why certain facets of your bond just seem to slot together easily.

But, of course, we're not always attracted to the people who make the easiest relationships for us, and if you find that the one you love rates only one or two stars, don't

8   7   6   5   4   3   2   1   9

give in! Challenges are often the 'meat' of a love affair – and all difficulties are somewhat soothed if you both share a birthday number in common, even if that number is derived from the *total* of the birth date rather than the actual DAY number. In other words, if your partner's LIFE number is the same as your DAY number, you will feel a pull towards each other which is very strong, even if the DAY numbers taken together have some wrinkles in their match-up. You will read more about this in the pages that follow the star chart.

The charts also include the master numbers **11** and **22**: these bring an extra dimension to relationships for those whose birth-number calculations feature either of these numbers at any stage. (For example, someone with a DAY number of **2** may be born on the 29th: 2+9 = **11**, and 1+1 = **2**. This means you should read the compatibility pairings for your number with both a **2** and an **11**.)

Sometimes the tensions that come to the surface in

9   1   2   3   4   5   6   7   8

love relationships are excellent for business relationships instead: the competitiveness that can undermine personal ties can accelerate effectiveness in working situations. We'll take a look at how other numbers match up with yours in vocational situations. And, when it comes to friends, you'll see why not all of your friendships are necessarily a smooth ride ...

In all matters – whether love, work or friendship – you will probably discover that the best partnerships you make involve an overlap of at least one number that you share in common. A number **9** attracts other number **9**s in various close ties throughout life.

NOTE: To satisfy your curiosity, ALL numbers are included in the star charts, so that you can check the compatibility ratings between your friends, co-workers and loved ones – and see why some relationships may be more turbulent than others!

| 8 | 7 | 6 | 5 | 4 | 3 | 2 | 1 | 9 |

Love

YOUR **LOVE** COMPATIBILITY CHART

	1	2	3	4	5
With a 1	★★★★	★★★★★	★★	★★★	★★★★★
With a 2	★★★★★	★★★★	★★★	★★★★★	★
With a 3	★★	★★★	★★★★★	★★	★★★★
With a 4	★★★	★★★★★	★★	★★★★	★★
With a 5	★★★★★	★	★★★★	★★	★★★
With a 6	★★★	★★★★	★★★★	★★★	★★
With a 7	★★★★★	★★	★★★	★★★★★	★★★
With an 8	★★★★	★★★★	★★★★★	★★★	★★★
With a 9	★★★	★★★	★★★★★	★★	★★★
With an 11	★★★★	★★★★	★★	★★★★★	★★
With a 22	★★★★	★★★★★	★★★	★★★★	★★★★

| 9 | 1 | 2 | 3 | 4 | 5 | 6 | 7 | 8 |

6	7	8	9	11	22
★★★	★★★★★	★★★★	★★★	★★★★	★★★★
★★★★	★★	★★★★	★★★	★★★★	★★★★★
★★★★	★★★	★★★★★	★★★★★	★★	★★★
★★★	★★★★★	★★★	★★	★★★★★	★★★★
★★	★★★	★★★	★★★	★★	★★★★
★★★★★	★	★★★	★★★★★	★★★★	★★★★
★	★★★	★★★★	★★★	★★★★	★★★★★
★★★	★★★★	★★★	★★	★★★★★	★★★★
★★★★★	★★★	★★	★★★	★★★★	★★★
★★★★	★★★★	★★★★★	★★★★	★★	★★★★★
★★★★	★★★★★	★★★★	★★★	★★★★★	★★

8	7	6	5	4	3	2	1	9

9 in love with a 1   ★★★

This love relationship can work particularly well, because **1** is a starter and you like to finish things off, if possible: a perfect harmony of wills. And, too, you have such a depth of vision regarding what may be possible that it inspires the **1**'s best energies and drives them forward with clever ideas. So far, all good. **1**'s originality gets a fine-tuning from you, and they respect you for being many things that they're not – as do you with them.

The wind blows across the emotional waters between you, however, when impatient **1** feels as though they are always in the driving seat and working hard to motivate you. On a good day, your moods are divine – for yours is a spiritual number, full of hope, of looking for what is good in others. But, on a down day, how can aggressive **1** motivate sensitive **9** to feel better? You go over and over the

9   1   2   3   4   5   6   7   8

things that upset you, never letting go of hurts from previous times, and **1** just wants to push forwards and make a new life.

On the credit side, you appreciate each other's very distinctive – and quite different – sense of humour, and your **1** enjoys the sympathy you give them ... the way you really listen ... the time you will take to please them ... the warmth and patience you exhibit, which is a balm for **1**'s haste and inner turmoil. You can have fun together, enjoying activities that some might see as childlike. You are both idealistic, and you can fall in love with dramatic depth of feeling, inspiring a loyalty in **1** which they truly long to give. And **1** likes the way others will seek you out for advice, to listen, because they know you are indeed both clever and (usually) wise. And you may be in awe of shining **1**'s single-mindedness and determined energies.

But if you have had a bumpy start in life – as many **9**s do – **1** will discover that there are two sides to your personality in love, and they won't know how to cope. Sometimes you are generous, and share your thoughts, but at other times you withdraw and lapse into self-interest. A **1** is too straight-up for this. Plus, you often create relationships that are odd or strange, with some demand from you of self-sacrifice. This is the least helpful character trait, when teamed with **1**'s propensity to be self-reliant and self-centred, for it will annoy and confuse them. And if you dwell for too long on any point, which is possible, **1** will lose patience with you, and the love will become strained.

The other critical problem – which may be more noticeable after time – is that you can be too indecisive for bombastic **1**'s taste. They know when and where they are going, and you may still be vacillating with bags packed and passport in hand. Or, **1** may find that dragging sensitive **9** out of dark spaces is not always easy, so they travel or go out alone. This self-will may grate on you.

9	1	2	3	4	5	6	7	8

Yet, if your combined energies – **1**'s courage, and **9**'s wisdom – can be directed well, you may be one of the happiest and most attractive couples on the planet. It hinges on how well your **1** can prompt you, without being too pushy!

Key themes

1 will take the lead, but **9** will finish whatever you start together • **9** brings out the artistic side of **1** better than anybody • **1** can help the **9** to discover greater self-confidence • **1** adds a bit of dash and genius to **9** 's real intelligence

| 8 | 7 | 6 | 5 | 4 | 3 | 2 | 1 | 9 |

9 in love with a 2   ★★★

Though only scoring three stars, this relationship may do well. 2s have an instinct with partnerships of all kinds, and 9s are loving souls in a 'cuddle-the-world' sort of way. 2 will be very impressed by the breadth of your thinking, and 9s have a way, too, of being good for 2s, making them feel better about themselves and increasing their self-confidence, because you listen to what they have to say – even encourage them to talk. This is especially true if the 2 is an 11: 9 feels for an 11, and they may be the one person who can prod you out of the abstract-thinking phase and into action.

Storms arise when you go negative, which happens not infrequently, for you sensitively mirror other people's feelings. This is hard on the 2, because they're not aggressive and will be more inclined to suffer alongside you than

| 9 | 1 | 2 | 3 | 4 | 5 | 6 | 7 | 8 |

issue ultimatums. **9**s also carry some serious emotional baggage from the past – concerning parents and past lovers – and may not always be able to extricate themselves from tangles. In fact, you somehow manage to get caught up in emotionally complicated relationships and draw compliant **2** in, as well – which may be fine if your intuitive **2** can play the no-nonsense counsellor, but this is rarely the case for a **2** when love is in the air!

But what does work well works very well. You broaden each other's horizons, and have a willingness to learn from one another; and you may goad **2** gently into disciplining their own good mind more than anyone else can. Add to this a pinch of seascape – because you are drawn to, and flourish by, the sea together – and an interest shared in words and reading or writing, and many good things could be borne of this relationship. You need a true companion, and **2** offers this: but they will need to allow you some personal freedom to go off alone, or with friends, for if your **2** is too cloying and demonstrates any insecurity, you will be frustrated and angry and lose your exceptional goodwill.

The way to make this relationship work is to take each other by the hand and find a cause to share – whether that is study, family, politics, or your children's education. When far-seeing **9** borrows **2**'s tact and diplomatic skill, anything can happen. And the personal relationship will prosper as long as **2** doesn't need constant reassurances that they're loved or being considered, for this will bore you. If they keep their sense of mystery, so that you're always wondering about them, you will keep each other enthralled.

On the positive side you will have a varied life, as **9** excites **2** to be more adventurous than usual. Some **2**s remain homebodies, but **9** will never settle for this, and needs fresh stimulation. This gives shy **2** more scope and helps them to grow. Part of what **2** finds so magnetic about you is your call to understand the world, and to explore what is not on the doorstep. **2** will go along with this and resign some quietness for the party lifestyle.

2, however, must be careful not to aggravate you about the past. Like **7**s, **9**s bottle up some emotions and reactions. Over time, if anyone can gain your trust it will be gentle **2**; but forcing the issue will create dramas. Then, the relationship may not take the strain. Gentleness and patience – which you both have – is required somewhere along the line, so be willing to let this bond find its own pace, and hope that your well-meaning **2** can go with it rather than trying to remould or redirect it. If they can do this, good things may unfold.

Key themes

9 will probably take the lead, but **2** assists and helps them finish what they start · Good understanding of people · Shared taste, to a degree – especially for literature, film and art · **9** needs emotional privacy about the past!

| 8 | 7 | 6 | 5 | 4 | 3 | 2 | 1 | 9 |

9 in love with a 3   ★★★★★

This relationship has scope for durability. **9** loves everything and everyone, and **3** invites the sometimes moody **9** into the world to play a little more often. If there is one special gift **3** brings to **9**, it's optimism, for you are often brought down by others' social flaws. **3** rolls with the punches far better, and has a very uplifting effect on **9**, which is vital. You also have many things in common. **3** is excited by your long list of talents and interests – in theatre and art, with words, with sounds. You broaden **3**'s vision, make them feel there are real possibilities in this world. This is good for talented **3**, because their awareness, though sharp, is often limited by what is familiar. You make them much more desirous of knowing a greater world.

Problems can arise when you become too negative: **3** has little time for gloom. **9** is the mirror number, reflecting

9   1   2   3   4   5   6   7   8

others strongly, losing its own identity and sense of self in the process. This isn't a problem if you are surrounded by bright spirits and laughing characters like joyful **3**, but, if you have a bad day at work, the clown in **3** will wonder why it brings you so low, and why you can't just get over it. Nothing is quite so simple for a **9** – and **3** may feel you make heavy weather of things that they'd simply shrug off. Also, you may be too sensitive to criticism for **3**'s liking.

This is just a brief caution, however. If **3** loves you, they must be prepared to get through some rainy days; but they won't be year-long, as yours is a number well able to listen to reason over time. If **3** can be patient, they should help you to recover your sunshine, and you can emerge together into warmth again. And this is well worth doing, because you see much more depth in your **3** than others allow. The trouble with being the class clown is that **3**'s sensitivities are either dismissed or ignored. You know how they feel inside, and help redirect their disappointment to take their creative dreams to fruition. In fact, no one does this better – for **9** sees real talent in **3**'s creativity.

In love you may be idealistic together, for there is a dreamy quality you share. You need to get **3** to concentrate on financial order, and to maximize your considerable joint earning potential through your gifts – which **3**s often fail to do themselves. Your gentleness is a co-operative partner to **3**'s giddiness and will show the way, introducing **3** to a range of ideas and experiences that are quite freeing. There will be arguments – often – but they may be generated by **3** more than you; you will simply retreat if the going gets too hard. Make sure flamboyant **3** is saying what they really mean, and not just speak for dramatic effect, for they will hurt you without complete awareness.

You know everyone, want to travel everywhere, are interested in everything, artistically and literally. **3** struggles to fit in all the interests they are drawn to, but will almost certainly push themselves to be successful – and not

9   1   2   3   4   5   6   7   8

just materially. You are more concerned with the things in life that touch the imagination or provoke serious thought, and this discipline is good for **3**. If anyone can convince them to take their skills that bit further, it will be you.

Alert the sometimes unthinking **3** to your wounds from past affairs and childhood, and don't accept any teasing about this. If **3** – with their carping humour – tries to take the lid off this potential Pandora's box, it may unleash more than you both bargained for. Always demand a little free time, and let **3** go off partying with other friends on occasion. Such generosity of spirit will be repaid.

Key themes

3 can turn **9**'s gloom into renewed hope, and respects **9**'s intelligence and depth • Co-operative partnership with much idealism • **9** inspires **3**'s best creative ideas and helps focus **3**'s energy

8   7   6   5   4   3   2   1   9

9 in love with a 4   ★★

This relationship demands a lot of flexibility from you – which you are able to give, but will need to do so regularly. Although there are many overlapping skills and character traits, it won't be easy-going to make it work every day. If the **4** has a developed talent for writing or creativity with their hands – which **4**s so often do – you might excite each other's creative talents well. **9** has such a way with words, and **4** looks up to you for your fine mind and variety of knowledge and interests. If **4** can learn from your wisdom and deep thinking, and you from **4**'s immediate inclination to find out how or why a thing can be done, both of you might fly high. **9**, though, is not always a tremendous finisher of what it starts, because so many new options evolve, and **4** will find this frustrating and become grumpy.

9	1	2	3	4	5	6	7	8

Metaphorically (if not physically) tall, and having the innate skills of a born actor, you enter a room and **4** is immune to the buzz. They've seen it all before, after all. But in deeper conversation, after the fuss dies down, **4** and **9** do find common ground. Your insights are a revelation to **4**, who is appreciative of someone who thinks deeply like this. Always wanting to know more, you seem like an encyclopedia of cultural thought. **4** is persuaded to reconsider long-held opinions on politics and society under the tutelage of a **9**. While they so often feel the need to keep their vision focused on the material and the present, you suggest there may be other ways to look at life – other ideas that are important, other skills to develop. But you may not be so keen to be held back by slower-thinking **4**'s earnest questions. **9** *feels* things; **4** prefers to reason them out. And this is going to be an obstacle.

Once the physical attraction dies down (and **4** can be derailed at times by a strong, earthy physical attraction!), these numbers may not be headed in the same direction. **9** desperately desires a life peppered with change and variety, while **4** is determined to batten down the hatches and prevent those winds of change from blowing through. Change is onerous for a **4**, but life's blood to a **9**. A recipe for trouble, then – at least, at times.

9s can be very idealistic about love, seeking a partner who inspires their creativity and their poetic soul. A **4** will hardly do this, as being earthy and sensible is what they respect. A life built on dreams is useless for them, and you are the ultimate dreamer. Of course, for a while this will fascinate them, and other qualities you possess certainly do inspire **4**'s feelings. **9** is warmer than **4**, has integrity and a great power to influence other people. You enjoy life and have a relaxed attitude about so many things, which can only be good for overworked, often insecure and more narrowly focused **4**. But if your **4** feels criticized they will retreat into their shell, and you are sometimes critical without being aware that you've said anything out of place.

But you are forgiving, which **4** appreciates; and they have a sound sense of values and a reliable character, which you need more than you admit. Both of you like to perfect what you do, and be known for a high standard of achievement. But your moody changeability may bother **4**, and they may never feel secure with you. And perhaps you find **4** too contrary and stubborn in the face of all argument. Not an easy alliance, this, but one that may give you ground for greater self-knowledge in the long run!

Key themes

4 resists 9's impulsiveness and wish to be close to so many diverse people · 9 feels tied down by 4 and unable to roam (metaphorically) · May accentuate each other's moodiness and 'self' focus

| 8 | 7 | 6 | 5 | 4 | 3 | 2 | 1 | 9 |

9 in love with a 5　　　★★★

With two numbers that are forever on the move, perhaps the attraction between you came about on a plane or in an international hotel? You may have glimpsed each other's smart luggage – which stood out from all others in the lobby – rather approvingly. Your taste is more conventional and traditional, but 5 can admire that, and also draw approbation from you for their own ineffable signature style. Part of the magnetism between these numbers, indeed, is about energy and movement, a sense of the *possible*, a wish for cramming life with activity, thought and feeling. The travellers personified of the number-cycle, **9** and **5** are both sensory and yet philosophical, and together you have much to interest one another on a day-to-day, and month-to-month, basis.

Where **5** wants stimulus, but has to fight many num-

9	1	2	3	4	5	6	7	8

bers to be allowed personal freedom and opportunity, you will certainly never hold them back or forbid them from trying things independently. You are excited by their forcefulness about life, their feeling that all experiences are for the trying. Most likely neither one of you will prejudge others because of the colour of their skin, their cultural creed, or their social status. **5**s and **9**s take anyone on merit, and are prepared to be enthralled by any other human being with a tale to tell.

These common humanitarian tenets are a strong draw-card in your potential relationship, and this is part of what works well. Both of you are also bright, wilful and alert. Just as importantly, **5** – with all the acumen and optimism of their number – is good for your sometimes moody and depressive side, taking you by the hand and leading you out of gloominess. And their versatility and talent for promotion can underwrite your abilities in the arts or educational arena. **9**s often prevaricate in life, with too many talents to choose from, but if anyone can make you feel your power and potential – and help you to utilize it – it will be **5**!

So why isn't it a five-star relationship? After **9** has been excited by **5**'s contacts and motoring power, a basic need to be a loner and live a quieter life at times may be at odds with **5**'s restlessness. You can be just *too* gloomy – feeling for the ills and pains of everyone else. **5** has no time for such sentiment, because their generosity and love is about positivity; **5** is always ready to work on cheering up a fellow life-passenger, but not going over and over the same ground. **9** can't make that cut-off point.

Then, too, in terms of expectation, **5** may be too much of a gambler for you: you want someone to concentrate on your needs. **9** is a missionary, a reformer, a person who is excited by achieving the wishes of others. This philanthropy may come at the expense of your relationship, and may leave **5** feeling a little too dull and worthy. Where's

9	1	2	3	4	5	6	7	8

the fun? But the worst problem is that neither of you has the steadiness to calm or direct the other's countless energies and creative gifts. **9** needs more of a rock than **5** can be, and **5** will appreciate a partner who can offer them space and wisdom. So, what is good is *good* between you – but the nervousness you may generate in each other could make a truly lasting relationship a little elusive.

Key themes

Both ready for change and variety in lifestyle and among friends • **9** is warm, spontaneous and unprejudiced; **5** can help **9** discover greater humour, self-expression and self-confidence • Both a little high-strung – **9** more a traditionalist, and **5** in a tearing hurry

8 7 6 5 4 3 2 1 9

9 in love with a 6   ★★★★★

This is potentially very powerful. You each have a goodness and a kindness which buoys and intensifies the other's. As a pair, you would be very giving and indulgent to friends in need or people who want your time. **6** helps **9** slow down and become very unselfish, while **9** forces **6** to think a little more deeply about their talents and interests, their future and what will make them happy. **6**'s failing is that it's often too easy-going or too much of a dilettante, but you have some of the force of personality to make your sweet **6** perfect their gifts a little.

And you are drawn to **6**: their taste, their looks, the way they appear to the world. With a shared enjoyment of music, theatre and art, you may even broaden **6**'s scope, for you are very much birds of a feather in this respect. You could inspire willing **6** to a greater love of literature, a wish to see the whole world rather than stay at home, and make them think about the politics and philosophies of cultures at a distance from their own. In return, **6** is able to make you a little less restless and sad, lifting your spirits after a stressful day. **9** is so prone to feel others' woes personally, and sensitive, kind **6** understands how to remedy some of this over-identification. Yet, **6**'s faith in you may indeed force you to pursue your wider ambitions, and together you could make a difference to the world, rather than just beautifying your own.

You can be very introspective at times, and **6** must cope with this, and not take it personally. And, as people-loving as **6** is, even they may find there are weekends when they don't want a trail of your mad friends traipsing through their door. **6** wants to make some time for love and tenderness, and needs to signal you to this effect. You are both dreamy, but you leave the world completely at times, leaving **6** wondering what they did or said.

8   7   6   5   4   3   2   1   9

Caught up in your subconscious, you may forget others' needs of you. Healing, sensitive, gentle, you are nonetheless cerebral sometimes, and ask **6**'s greatest patience. If your **6** is a strong home-maker – common to many **6**s – they'll have to accept that a happy home with a **9** requires a back door left unlatched, so you can wander in when you have finished wandering elsewhere. You're not disloyal or a player, but you don't like to feel restricted: **9**s are actors, and their world has many stages. Anyone in love with a **9** has to learn to tolerate – even enjoy – these various roles.

But let's be honest: this is what drew **6** to you in the first place. You are so seductive to them, needing love, resisting labels, refusing to be 'normal', yet utterly charming and versatile and high-minded. How can **6** resist such appeal – youthfulness wrapped up in a wise old mind? And, even when they're obstinate and a little jealous, how can you be immune to their beautifying touches and serene engagement with people and life? You like mutual

9   1   2   3   4   5   6   7   8

things, prefer the truth from one another, and can learn from each other. When **6** is feeling stay-at-home, they will suggest you go visit a friend out of town.

If the love between you grows to a lasting tie and you have children, **6** must remember your *personal* needs. **6** often gets tied up with those who need them, children being a prime concern, but you need them too. Keep the relationship precious and give it plenty of air – away from others. Walking and talking together, listening to each other, is one of the things about this match that can work so well. If you lose it, you lose something very unique.

Key themes

A partnership that can really lead to *love* • **9** is intelligent, warm and broad-minded, enlarging **6**'s world • **6** is patient and loving, beautifies **9**'s world, and offers gentle security • Shared interests and compatible styles

8   7   6   5   4   3   2   1   9

9 in love with a 7 ★★★

With your tremendous charm and rich imagination, and your appreciation of arts and ideas, **9** strongly appeals to picky **7**. Together you have a powerful sympathy and feeling for other people, but you are also a good companion and a fun-loving yet intelligent friend, and this is important to a **7**. You may be able to make **7** laugh when no one else can, being a natural actor and having a good, facile mind; **7** sometimes needs to be chivvied out of too much self-analysis, and you can do this. **7** will be drawn to you, in fact, largely because you are willing and able to stand up to them. **7** can be so high-handed with other mortal thinkers, often unintentionally, but you won't stand for this arrogance – and won't take offence, either. Excellent medicine for arrogant-seeming **7**.

A **7** can share deeply probing conversations with you,

9	1	2	3	4	5	6	7	8

as you each have a love of literature and good expression, of film, and of the arts generally. You will approve of their discerning mind, and when we speak of **7** having a 'desert island' mentality, where only a privileged few may be invited, **9** is certainly one of those guests with a pass to virtually all areas. You even exceed a **7**'s distaste for small-minded and over-materialistic people and situations, and you two may be witty critics of cultural faux pas together.

So, again, why only three stars? Part of the problem is that you can be very idealistic and a bit over-indulgent about your personal life and emotional stresses, while **7** expects more grown-up behaviour, not prone personally to bleeding publicly if there's a problem. And you may possibly fall in love with a little too much gusto for a **7**'s taste: **7**s are always excited by the understated, the enig-matic, the hard-to-get. Both of you are dreamers, but a **9**'s dreams are based on idealism and a **7**'s on spirituality. There is excellent ground between you two for friendship

| 8 | 7 | 6 | 5 | 4 | 3 | 2 | 1 | 9 |

and a positive love affair, but promises of the great here-after may not suit, for you are ultimately going in different directions.

Once the sexual attraction quietens, **7** will become frustrated with you – the jack of many trades but rarely quite enough of a master of any of them to the satisfaction of fussy, perfectionist **7**. This may seem a small and even amusing warning, but over time it will grate. **9**s don't like being goaded too far, or asked to gift their good grace indefinitely without something in return. Though genuinely in awe of **7**'s poise and personal dignity, you fear clever **7** can also be too selfish – and there is some justice in this. **9** is a big brother to the world, where **7** is proud and a little reserved. These essential characteristics can lead to difficulties in the everyday mechanics of the relationship.

What definitely works is the high intelligence and respect for bigger ideas you each have, and this includes a thrill you get from reading and talking deeply, pondering the best way to achieve joy and social justice. What is not so good is the fact that **9** is an endearing grown-up child, full of enthusiasm and responsive emotions, whereas **7** is a born parent, middle-aged at five! Sympathies exist between you, and your hearts and souls are in the right place. If the mystical elements in your personalities are dominant, then the three-star rating may seem a little mean. The bond is better if you are older, perhaps.

Key themes

Shared depth of feeling and hopes of harmony for the world and its people, but **9** more people-orientated than **7** · **7** wishes **9** would be less like a bouncing puppy occasionally, while **9** would like **7** to loosen up!

| 8 | 7 | 6 | 5 | 4 | 3 | 2 | 1 | 9 |

9 in love with an 8 ★★

This is an excellent relationship for two people who want to share much of their life together. 9 is at home with 8's good mind and exceptional optimism that everything will come out fine in the end. 8 loves 9's genuine good humour and tolerance for all people – though at times they may think you a little too undiscerning or forgiving, and feel that some of your friends aren't worth the investment of time! 8 is definitely more hard-nosed than 9. But you both have an excellent imagination, and a good attitude towards broader life – recognizing that the world is much bigger than the space which simply surrounds the two of you.

If you are both interested in research or science and factual information (highly likely), you will excite one another and share hours of joy investigating what pleases you. You are both altruistic and have a philanthropic view

| 9 | 1 | 2 | 3 | 4 | 5 | 6 | 7 | 8 |

of the world and the people around you. **9** is lucky, well-read, and has a rounded personality, while **8** has a passion for the spiritual and metaphysical questions about life; and you will rove with them into pastures of exploration. Together you may be modernists or medievalists, but you will each be able to make the jump into the other's world.

9 lends **8** much creative thought and lots of ideas, and **8** brings to lofty but often unfocused **9** a power and concentration that may be lacking. **8** is much more geared to a real and practical life than you; but you can – and will – teach them to relax and make some personal demands. **8**, in some sense, can be happy and fulfilled by a **9** in a way that may be difficult with other numbers – and this is partly because you are both higher thinkers and somewhat free from social restraints. Both **8** and **9** are spiritual numbers in the most ecumenical sense – neither of you weighted down by tradition or expectation – and, as lovers, this can be very liberating and exciting.

8   7   6   5   4   3   2   1   9

Your **8** will truly love your universalist way of thinking: life is full of surprises with such a soul – a child and yet the most mature person they know. **8**, equally, gently places your feet back on the planet when you need grounding – which is not infrequently. A truly enlightened **9** can represent all that is beautiful in the human spirit – musical and artistic, kind and charitable – and this can sometimes make you idealistic, and wishing for perfection. The reality of life can be heartbreaking, and here **8**'s powerhouse character can come to the rescue. They have the magic formula of being able to hold on to one good thing and make it resonate across the bleaker moors of daily struggle, and you need this. Thus, as lovers, you can be like a pair of finely balanced acrobats, creating poetry and fluidity between earth and air.

So why is it, then, that this relationship rates a meagre two stars on the compatibility chart? The answer is that this bond – and it is a powerful one – is a little lacking

9   1   2   3   4   5   6   7   8

in romance, not very sensual. If you want a relationship with someone who could be a great friend, someone from whom you will learn and arguably never grow bored with, then it is worth following up the first date. But the danger is that it all may be a little businesslike, and that your sense of fun may not get much exercise. Of course, a friendship/love affair is very grown-up, and has the longevity that passionate flings rarely attain. It ultimately comes down to what you want; but if this love starts, you will go on – at least as lifelong friends – well past the point where most other pairs can run out of steam!

Key themes

May be more about friendship and business than love •
Similar mind-sets, and shared interest in a diverse number
of cultural and intellectual outlets • **9** calms **8**, and **8** puts
9 into a higher gear • Travel may feature strongly

| 8 | 7 | 6 | 5 | 4 | 3 | 2 | 1 | 9 |

9 in love with a 9   ★★★

Here is an interesting relationship – two people with a specialized and heightened view of the world who will keep each other on their toes. Romantic and loving one minute, cool and impersonal the next, you may confuse each other with your fluctuations of mood, even though you are both prone to it. Another **9** will certainly understand you very well, feel for you, recognize so much about you that they share too. But there is just no denying the habit **9** forms of getting in deeply, and then – unaccountably – going walkabout and wishing for space. Then everything is steamy and close again. This may create a frisson of excitement and adventure for a while, but it is likely to make you both crazy at times, too.

Arguably, two **9**s locked in a love affair may join to make the world around them a better place. One could envisage two parents on the school committee, regularly putting in their time and care for not only their own, but other people's children, improving the library and the school cuisine, offering to chaperone the trips, extending the range of clubs and visiting speakers in a truly exciting way. Within the community around you both, chez vous will be a haven of thought and discussion, a refuge for anyone in distress, a perfect address to crash at after a night of films and clubbing. Two **9**s will adopt their friends and their friends' friends. And oh, those weekend romantic breaks – depending on whose turn it is for the treat. One would take the other anywhere for a change of air.

So why doesn't this rate higher than the regular three stars? It comes down to the trouble from the past, and the moods. Another **9** will come with as much baggage as you have. They are forgiving, kind, vulnerable while appearing sound, certainly; but two **9**s might outdo one another for sadness, each feeling distraught about the condition of the world, the faithlessness of people, the insensitivity of even the best of friends. Someone needs to be jolly and buoy the other one up – and neither of you can be relied on to do this. That capacity you both have for feeling so acutely for the nearest and dearest in your lives would be fine-tuned to each other, and when one of you feels low, the other will want to join them in empathetic despair ...

Of course, this won't always be true, and when you are focused on the wider community you will use your clear-sightedness and intuition to brilliant effect, gaining some degree of enlightenment from each other. But humour is something you reflect and, when another soul makes you feel lively and bouncy, you return it with interest. Two **9**s may not be able to get outside themselves quite enough to let this spark ignite their better sides.

So, this can be great if good, then ... but lethal, if not. You're soulmate friends, perhaps, almost more so than ideal lovers.

9	1	2	3	4	5	6	7	8

Key themes

Both humanitarians, and a deep bond will grow stronger over time • Romance perhaps unstable, thanks to moodiness and stubbornness • Highs and lows

9 in love with an 11   ★★★★

We have already looked at your relationship with a pure **2** (*see page 140*), but what does it mean if the **2** happens to also be master number **11** (born on the 11th or 29th of the month)? Is this likely to improve things, or make them worse? The master numbers have a different impact on relationships ...

An **11** lover will give you quite a lift! You both have a wider sense of the world than your individual limits of interest, and will inspire each other to take steps that should be taken both socially and culturally. While two other numbers may just sit back and watch, an **11** partnering you will help you to feel that anything, and everything, is possible to achieve. And when it comes to loving, this relationship works very well. An **11** makes you giggle and knows how to divert you when you are feeling under siege from other people's expectations; and, likewise, you can get an **11** to take a step back and see the world with a touch more humour when it counts. **11** can be too driven, and not take a long enough pragmatic look at the circumstances to evaluate what needs doing before diving in. This, you can do for them.

Sometimes **11**'s ego will bother you – but only enough to make you laugh out loud, encouraging them to laugh in turn. Who else would dare laugh at an **11**? *This* is why you are so good for them. And, as a lover, they have magnetism, intelligence, and a very distinct style that makes you dream your most colourful dreams, firing up your most vivid imagination. You will make the **11** grow up a little – for they are so often like high-IQ children who are intolerant of others and desperately in need of a higher boredom threshold. But the **11** pays you in kind, helping you to work for a good cause and increasing your own personal momentum in life. It is the sense of possibility and humour and vivacity turned on life that excites you. This is a key relationship.

If you feel your **11** is being offhand or too emotional, you will tell them; and, when you are wallowing over a slight too much, they will surely let you know. You are paddling together in a very sleek canoe, navigating rapids, avoiding rocks and spills, and your adrenaline will pump to let you know you're truly alive. And in love.

This is a thrilling relationship, in all truth, and what you may do with your lives if you can both be at your best — driven, intelligent, determined, courageous — is waiting to be told. Not that every day will be meek and tender, or gentle and cuddly, but there will be such moments, and you would be living half of your life together if that was all. This is a roller-coaster ride, but a fascinating and generally enthralling one.

9   1   2   3   4   5   6   7   8

Key themes

Daring and high-voltage relationship • Sexually charged •
Full of ideas and lived in the fast lane • Magnetic around
people, achieving an exhilarating feeling of a colourful life

8   7   6   5   4   3   2   1   9

9 in love with a 22 ★★★

If you meet a love born on the 22nd of the month, you will know you have met someone special – an out-of-the-ordinary individual who is just the kind of person to excite your senses. Quietly dynamic in a crowd, fully independent and rather enigmatic, this person is going to whet your appetite for a life that knows no bounds. A **22** may want to travel more even than you do, and you love the way they have a quiet confidence in their ability, the way they walk into any situation ready to accept responsibility. That can be a heady aphrodisiac, for you meet so few people who have such charisma and substance with it.

So, your **22** love has more understanding of the ordinary world than many a **9**, and they are called to do something powerful in this life; but they may appear too earthed or materialistic to you, for in many ways their question of

9	1	2	3	4	5	6	7	8

spirituality is more rational than yours. You could be disappointed that your electric 22 thinks only of getting the job at hand done brilliantly, with romance taking a back seat. They appear so diplomatic and efficient, which indeed they are; but where does this leave their personal life? Many a 22 seems to sacrifice private concerns and wishes for greater duty. They take control so naturally, and are willing to perform any service when required for someone they believe is truly in need. Only rarely does this unusual soul become mired in personal strife and worldly concerns, but power does seem to wind up in their hands.

All of this will make you feel a compulsion to know, love and aid them; and if it does work, and you are both mature and have worked off the personal dramas that are likely to have made your earlier relationships difficult, then you may give each other a lot more return than the three stars in the chart suggest. But maybe 22 is too careful for you, on balance, worrying about things that seem too abstract for your taste. Money matters are a reality for a **22**, and it will irritate you. Your natural generosity may seem called into question, or you may feel that you are being judged for being quite so feeling of others – because **22** can feel without bleeding, always keeping their head on straight.

It is certainly a fascinating pairing, this, but ultimately **22** may make you too constrained to do what seems practical and possible – with a kind of 'let's get a reality check' approach. This may be good for you, but it may also limit you. You, after all, create your own reality. You are more of a drama king or queen, an arts soul – and **22** has a scientific approach to life, even when they are creative. **22** is a master architect – what numerology so often calls the 'master builder'; but **9** is the person who turns ice cream into castles. There is a clash of view. Have a fling is perhaps the best advice; looking for something more permanent might be frustrating.

9	1	2	3	4	5	6	7	8

Key themes

High minds with broad concerns but different approaches to problems • **22** may seem too proud for affable **9**, and **9** too flexible for strong **22** • Rapport and attraction, but day-to-day difficulties to be overcome

8 7 6 5 4 3 2 1 9

Work

YOUR **WORK** COMPATIBILITY CHART

	1	2	3	4	5
With a 1	★★★★	★★★★★	★	★★★	★★★
With a 2	★★★★★	★★★	★★★	★★★★	★
With a 3	★	★★★	★★★★	★★	★★★★★
With a 4	★★★	★★★★	★★	★★★★★	★★★
With a 5	★★★	★	★★★★★	★★★	★★
With a 6	★★	★★★★★	★★★★	★★★★	★★★★
With a 7	★★★★★	★★★	★★★	★★★★★	★★
With an 8	★★★★★	★★★★★	★★★★★	★★★	★★★★
With a 9	★★★★	★★★	★★★★★	★★	★★★
With an 11	★★	★★★★	★★★	★★★★★	★★
With a 22	★★★★★	★★	★★★	★★★	★★★★

9   1   2   3   4   5   6   7   8

6	7	8	9	11	22
★★	★★★★★	★★★★★	★★★★	★★	★★★★★
★★★★★	★★★	★★★★★	★★★	★★★★	★★
★★★★	★★★	★★★★★	★★★★★	★★★	★★★
★★★★	★★★★★	★★★	★★	★★★★★	★★★
★★★★	★★	★★★★	★★★	★★	★★★★
★★★	★	★★★★	★★★	★★★★★	★★★★
★	★★★★	★★★	★★	★★★★	★★★★★
★★★★	★★★	★★★	★★★★	★★★★★	★★★★
★★★	★★	★★★★	★★★	★★★★★	★★★★★
★★★★★	★★★★	★★★★★	★★★★★	★★★★	★★★★★
★★★★	★★★★★	★★★★	★★★★★	★★★★★	★★★

8	7	6	5	4	3	2	1	9

9 working with a 1   ★★★★

A pair of well-met souls at the office. **1** has the kind of forcefulness and optimism that helps you get out of bed on a stressful day, and you have the overall clarity to see how to turn **1**'s business ideas into actualities. **1** starts well, and you finish for them once they lose interest! Best of all, you create a feeling of goodness in the people who work around you, for **9**s keep **1**s in high spirits, while **1**s stop **9**s from worrying overly. And what good ideas you come up with together!

A **1** has a way of knowing exactly what you have to offer – perhaps more so than you. Time and again **1** will pick out the one diamond from the bag of crystals which pours metaphorically from your creative imagination; but, equally, you can put the **1**'s feelings into words for others. You will mimic them, but they'll see the funny side; no other number tends to get away with as much as you. You also both share a flair for the dramatic, and you will have fun teaming up for any promotional work or public relations exercises that come into your business's needs.

All **1**s have the talent to produce something original, which **9** can, in turn, make useful as well. All **9**s like to be of service to other people, and neither of you will be happy if confined to menial tasks, so together you are likely to break out of the humdrum, and create excitement around you. And if ever someone has to plead your case for you, to another audience or critic, **1** can do it – as you can for them. You grasp how a **1** does things, and are inclined to play along with even their maddest schemes!

Key themes

Rally each other's spirits • Starter teamed with finisher • Intuit one another's best gifts for work

8   7   6   5   4   3   2   1   9

9 working with a 2   ★★★

Together **2** and **9** are rowing in the same direction. **9** assumes a patriarchal protectiveness of **2**, but with good intentions, and **2** understands this, refusing to take offence. And sensitive **2** gently assuages **9**'s doubts about what is possible, pushing you to strive for the best (which is considerable). Often it is only disorganization that prevents **9**s from flying high, and **2** easily offsets this by taking care of details and filling in behind the **9**, who can be a showman, while keeping everyone calm and happy. **2** often helps **9** finish projects others have set in motion, and both of you create an atmosphere of ease for the people who work around you. You keep **2** feeling upbeat, and **2** prevents you from worrying unduly about what may never happen. Countering **9**'s potential for negativity is a great **2** skill.

The **2** also senses which of your dreams can become

realities and which are pie in the sky – a distinction you can't always make. As repayment, you verbalize **2**'s tender feelings of what may be contributed, for **2**s are never their own best press agents. You get on with almost everyone, and your approach to life can expand **2**'s social conscience. Work-wise, you will find the most productive way of tackling problems from sheer willingness to do so.

You will sometimes annoy **2**, mainly when they feel situations could be handled more efficiently. They may also feel cross that you want to be too many things to too many people, failing to concentrate on what you could do so well. But if anyone can smooth out these difficulties and show you where to put your energies, that person is **2**.

Key themes

Complementary talents • **9**'s moodiness confuses **2** • **2** gets on board with **9**'s plans

| 8 | 7 | 6 | 5 | 4 | 3 | 2 | 1 | 9 |

9 working with a 3 ★★★★★

This is another potentially good working partnership, as both of you know how to work hard when the mood takes you and when you are feeling motivated. **9** and **3** both have such vivid imaginations, and together you find many ways to repackage old ideas and make them more modern and relevant. **9**'s moral integrity, too, will be refreshing for **3**, as they often feel that subordinates are given either unfair treatment or not enough credit for what they do. Under the direction of a **9**, life is kinder for everyone.

Moreover, a **3** can always out-talk a **9** (not usually easy!), and win a point for other people who have something to say. You will listen to a **3**, and do them the courtesy of heeding their advice, knowing it is based on sharp instinct. **3** also has a way of making the sometimes over-serious **9** see the funny side of a situation. Together, you

| 9 | 1 | 2 | 3 | 4 | 5 | 6 | 7 | 8 |

will disarm your adversaries or competition, and walk away with the prize everyone was seeking!

Go into the travel, theatrical, publishing or even underwear business together: you have the facility of recognizing where the world is going and what it needs to entertain and equip it on the way. You both genuinely like people, and this means you can feel your time is well spent on any outlet which caters for people. This is distinctly different from the mind-set of a **7**, perhaps, or a **1**, both of whom like to work in isolation, and who get it right – where the public's taste is concerned – almost as a matter of mediation. **3** and **9** know, upfront and personal, how people feel. You feel it with them.

Key themes

Understand the public's taste • Work in tandem • Good humour and amenable relationships with others

| 8 | 7 | 6 | 5 | 4 | 3 | 2 | 1 | 9 |

9 working with a 4   ★★

Not a work relationship made in heaven, this! **9** is such a dilettante, to **4**'s mind, unable to concentrate on one thing long enough to exact a result. And, to **9**, **4** is such a stickler, always holding others up with questions that seem impossibly literal. As a number working at its best level, **9** is the conceptualist with a focus on the broader community – a universalist with an inclination to think metaphorically. This is far too abstract for sensible **4**, who wonders what planet you came from. Stability and willingness to accept responsibility are a byword in **4**'s character, but you seem to view these traits with near-contempt. Always seeking freedom, you may appear to be too flaky or aspirant for **4**. Yet, there is sometimes space for success, too.

A well-educated and experienced **9** gains wisdom in a short time, learning from problems first time round. You

| 9 | 1 | 2 | 3 | 4 | 5 | 6 | 7 | 8 |

understand how to attain the highest goals, driven by a need to complete and perfect whatever you take up. When at the top of your game you're able to enlist a lot of confidence from everyone around you – and earthy **4** will be exactly the ally to help. With their methodical approach to the impossible, together you may reach out to the wider world, and, no matter how many difficulties you encounter, it is the sense and rectitude of **4** that makes a difference. **9** can be a dreamer, but **4** has no time for idle wishes. If something is to be done **4** will do it, and the friendship of a **9**, once won, is there forever. Tensions will definitely exist, and tempers may flare. It all depends on how strongly the positive traits of both numbers dominate between you.

Key themes

One works from method, the other from metaphor • Joy or despair dictated by willingness to be positive

| 8 | 7 | 6 | 5 | 4 | 3 | 2 | 1 | 9 |

9 working with a 5 ★★★

At the office, **5** is the 'people person' and **9** the feeling humanitarian who understands colleagues' woes. What motivates each of you may be diverse: **5** is curious, spontaneous and warm, finding joy in communicating with people from all walks of life; **9** is broad-minded, compassionate and altruistic, always anxious to please others. **9**s set high standards and **5** might respond to this.

Like **1**, **5** has the kind of optimism that helps you get out of bed on a stressful day, while you have the clarity to see how to realize **5**'s business ideas. And you finish what the **5** started, once they lose interest. You buoy **5**'s spirits while they stop you from stressing unduly, and together you produce excellent ideas – though you will need others to do the administration! Your head is full of so much, and **5** has a way of being quite cold-blooded with others'

| 9 | 1 | 2 | 3 | 4 | 5 | 6 | 7 | 8 |

frantic ideas in a way they can never achieve on their own. A **5** may see plainly when your head is too high in the clouds, and they're the one person fearless enough to say so. **5** is the force needed to get you out of the blocks – preventing you from over-rehearsing each performance.

But arguments and aggravation will scatter **5**'s energies, and the two of you may run headlong into the more negative traits of your numbers, and lose confidence or feel blocked. Acknowledge the need for discipline, and adhere to the sequential processing rule that there must be a beginning, middle and end to achieve a strong result. Have a plan and a budget, and stick to it. Keep a sense of adventure in what you do, and define your direction.

Key themes

An energized team • Intuit one another's best gifts for work • Employ a management team to polish your efforts

| 8 | 7 | 6 | 5 | 4 | 3 | 2 | 1 | 9 |

9 working with a 6   ★★★

Probably better suited to a personal relationship than a business tie, the interaction between your two numbers is nevertheless still very positive, and offers a chance for each of you to work at your best individual capacity. 6 won't interfere with 9's lofty thinking and forward-planning, nor will 9 forget the niceties that make 6 feel comfortable in a work atmosphere. 6 will always feel consulted by 9, and has much to say. In one sense, 9 has mastery over the words and 6 over the visions; 6 has the ability to see how an end product or service should be presented to the world, but 9 knows whether it has any potential. In tandem, this is good.

You will always make 6 feel valued as a negotiator, and will help them to see their own ability at a higher level. 6s so often let opportunities float away through mild lack of

| 9 | 1 | 2 | 3 | 4 | 5 | 6 | 7 | 8 |

ambition or conflict with personal obligations, but you won't stand for this, and will ask them to learn anything their training may be missing, in order to go up a level.

When it comes to calming down after a stressful situation – perhaps a tricky client or peer group – or a busy day, **6** performs the magic for you. A **9** can really feel personally 'wrung out' from difficult conditions, but a **6** has a soothing manner and a good philosophical spin on day-to-day things. In a nutshell, **6** makes daily life at 'the office' more comfortable for **9**, allowing them to think and plan, while **9** ponders the direction in the longer term, and asks for **6**'s gracious companionship in the journey ahead. A very sensible and well-mannered arrangement.

Key themes

Understand what the public wants and how to provide it
• Share a love of life outside the office • Good friendship

| 8 | 7 | 6 | 5 | 4 | 3 | 2 | 1 | 9 |

9 working with a 7 ★★

This is more likely to stifle each partner's creative and intellectual powers than propel you to business paradise. **9** wants to be in charge of – and try out – many things, but this is against **7**'s nature: **7**s become positively scathing about anyone trying their hand if they are not a specialist trained for the job. **9** is more relaxed with others, and **7** may seem too isolated and content in their own space. While both numbers seek inner truths and personal growth in life generally, you have different ways of attacking this objective. Business-wise, **9** is restless and prefers to travel, while **7** likes to concentrate on achieving the best that can be, and not move on until that has been reached. Plus, **7** tires of **9**'s emotional life spilling into the office: they keep their emotions on a tight leash, and wonder how you can be so casual about your intimate life.

9	1	2	3	4	5	6	7	8

On the other hand, there is a good meeting of minds if the business direction is artistic or humanitarian in any way – science or medicine, literature or the arts. Then, you may work peaceably, without cut-throat techniques. And your understanding of what makes others work will help immeasurably. Your combined talents could offer a cushion of wisdom for those around you.

Success or failure depends on how much respect you develop for each other, and what field you operate in. You admire 7's mind and self-motivation, but worry about their sharp tongue. If you can find a way past these blocks, there may be something excellent to uncover in a business relationship. But agree to do things very differently.

Key themes

Contrasting styles: **7** a perfectionist, **9** interested in many outlets for their talents • Works best in arts or sciences

8   7   6   5   4   3   2   1   9

9 working with an 8   ★★★★

As a **9**, you possess an excellent imagination and a strong vision: an **8** can harness that vision and paint something masterly. With a flair for the dramatic and the absurd, you can recover some of **8**'s playfulness, and bring a wonderful balance between success and pleasure into the work arena.

You are both showmen, with a feeling for the spectacular, paying detailed attention to the impact everything may have on a client or in the marketplace. **9**s have an essential talent in many creative fields, but not always the best organizational skills or an understanding of their own clever ideas. **8** can remedy this pretty smartish, showing the often distracted **9** how to assemble such a plethora of gifts into a manageable and desirable package or product.

Whatever business you happen to work in – and best if it is in either a creative or a political landscape – think of

| 9 | 1 | 2 | 3 | 4 | 5 | 6 | 7 | 8 |

the marriage of **8** and **9** in business as the entrepreneur (**8**) seeing the opportunities around the performer/actor (**9**). This will apply even if your vocational domain is in science or medicine. **8** must direct and manage your talent; and, if you drop into a moody state or become depressed (as often happens), who do you suppose can chivvy you out of it? **8** has the power like no other number to achieve constructive material accomplishments which also have an altruistic or socially responsible edge, and you will blossom under such tutelage. **8** is often a force to be seen to be believed, but can become a slave to their intellect sometimes. You can help them recover some much-needed feeling, and together you could discover pleasure and prosperity.

Key themes

Profitable curiosity, with different ways of seeing • Blend of feeling, courage and sense • Makes good business

| 8 | 7 | 6 | 5 | 4 | 3 | 2 | 1 | 9 |

9 working with a 9   ★★★

If the business is showbiz-related in any way, be prepared for the scale of the operation to grow quickly: two **9**s heighten each other's imagination, wit, people skills and *joie de vivre* brilliantly. You both have great energy and intelligence, ask all the right questions, have the capacity to motivate and inspire everyone around you. Two **9**s in business will see everything through to a brilliant conclusion and make sure that anything you do together feels right, is fun and has an application for society which in some way – however small – improves other people's lots.

What will work very well is the innate communication: you will each understand what the other is thinking, or feeling, before the clock strikes ten. This is excellent in any meeting or situation where a client might be involved – rather like having the perfect doubles partner at tennis,

| 9 | 1 | 2 | 3 | 4 | 5 | 6 | 7 | 8 |

who knows just what you're likely to do and how you think.

But the rating of only three stars (which is still good, though) is because you may also exaggerate each other's weaknesses. Two **9**s will consider every option, bring too many different aspects of work into play, not concentrate solely on the achievement of one small goal at a time. And, two **9**s may not be cold-blooded enough about the material aspects of work, trusting to luck or hoping that others you deal with will be honourable. If you can find a third party who is an **8** or a master number, all will be well; but **9**s alone may be unable to stabilize each other's moods on down days, and refuse to go for the kill – even if it is ultimately in the best interests of many people.

Key themes

Good humour and strong intuition · Moodiness and worry can work against you · Success depends a little on others

| 8 | 7 | 6 | 5 | 4 | 3 | 2 | 1 | 9 |

9 working with an 11   ★★★★★

You work very well with an **11**. What works with a **2** goes up a notch with this master-number bond. Adding **9** and **11** we come to **20**, or **2**: partners. Together, these numbers are co-operative, inspired, have wonderfully uplifting energies on the people around them, and like to get things done with style and sunshine laughter. As a team, you can assert yourselves in turn – **11** doing so most of the time, but you, as the **9**, holding them back from too much impatience with others. Your partnership seems to make magical things happen, and to bring secrets to light. What might your business be?

Whatever you do, surely people are involved? You are so good together at taking meetings and creating sparkling conversations, so PR and any work which advertises or merchandises products will be perfect for you. You are both full of hopes and ambitions – perhaps **11** having more of the sheer ambition, and you adding in that vital element of hope. You bring a necessary quality of diplomacy to the table, and the results are that you can sell beef to a vegetarian restaurant or British fashion in France. On top of this, you bring out the best of **11**'s wit, and you make a dazzling pair with a very bright sense of what can be done ... and how to do it.

Any cautions? Try to urge the **11** to be cautious sometimes about who to talk to, or how much to say. You will have a feeling about this, and if you pay attention to your instincts you could achieve miracles at work with this clever master number.

Key themes

Humour, vitality, intellect and good people skills help you see endless possibilities and stay ahead of the crowd

| 8 | 7 | 6 | 5 | 4 | 3 | 2 | 1 | 9 |

9 working with a 22　　★★★★★

22 knows how to weave straw into gold, and you will learn from this. Much of what we have just said about your relationship with an **11** is true again here: you are able to bounce off one another and create a good working relationship. The **22** is a wonderful business number anyway – highly trained to think altruistically and understand that cash is needed for anything charitable. You will respond to this. The result is that you will marry your wishes and intellects, and arrive together at a work achievement that benefits many and is guaranteed to give you a lifestyle you'll enjoy – allowing you to be generous and to travel, and to work at something which has meaning for you both.

Rest assured that a **22** sees to it that the accounts are done properly, the tax returns filed, and the flow charts prepared. The IT department will have constant service and upkeep, and even if your business is arts-related you will manage it with precision. You have the potential together to accrue wealth and win people's confidence.

Government work might attract you both, working for the greater good of the community or country you live in; and, again, there is an air of showbiz about the style you will employ to get the job done. What is vital is that a **22** will tie you down a little, and teach you to think about business professionally. This frees you, then, to delve deep into your considerable swag of talents, and do something that cheers the soul and makes a success. Bliss! Don't be frightened to say if the **22** is being egotistical or too self-reliant. Make them share!

Key themes

22 takes 'masterly' lead, which **9** won't mind • **9** can help **22** relax and open up • Both very original and ethical

8   7   6   5   4   3   2   1   9

Friendship

YOUR **FRIENDSHIP** COMPATIBILITY CHART

	1	2	3	4	5
With a 1	★★★	★★★★★	★★	★★★	★★★
With a 2	★★★★★	★★	★★★	★★★★	★
With a 3	★★	★★★	★★★★	★	★★★★
With a 4	★★★	★★★★	★	★★★★★	★★
With a 5	★★★	★	★★★★	★★	★★★
With a 6	★	★★★★	★★★★★	★★★	★★★★
With a 7	★★★★	★★★★★	★★★★	★★★★★	★
With an 8	★★★★	★★★★	★★★★★	★★	★★★★
With a 9	★★★★	★★★	★★★★	★★★★	★★★★
With an 11	★★★	★★★★★	★★	★★★★★	★★
With a 22	★★★	★★★	★★★★	★★	★★★

9   1   2   3   4   5   6   7   8

6	7	8	9	11	22
★	★★★★	★★★★	★★★★	★★★	★★★
★★★★	★★★★★	★★★★	★★★	★★★★★	★★★
★★★★★	★★★★	★★★★★	★★★★	★★	★★★★
★★★	★★★★★	★★	★★★★	★★★★★	★★
★★★★	★	★★★★	★★★★	★★	★★★
★★★★	★	★★★★	★★★★	★★★	★★★★★
★	★★★★	★★★	★★	★★★★★	★★★★★
★★★★	★★★	★★★★	★★★★	★★★★★	★★★
★★★★	★★	★★★★	★★	★★★★	★★★★
★★★	★★★★★	★★★★★	★★★★	★★★★★	★★★★
★★★★★	★★★★★	★★★	★★★★	★★★★	★★

8	7	6	5	4	3	2	1	9

Always at your best in social gatherings, you find friends in the most unconventional places — though some expand your mind more than others! Let's see which are the best combinations ... and which are the worst:

9 and 1 (★★★★): **9** gets on with everyone really (the lowest star rating is only a two), and with the number **1** you have a lot of fun together and make a good balance for each other's energies. **1** can be selfish, but you won't stand for that, and know how to call their bluff.

9 and 2 (★★★): Also a good friendship, though you may find **2** a little too tame sometimes. You like their intuition and kind spirit, but now and again it will drive you mad that they don't push themselves forward a little more. Perhaps you will help them?

9 and **3** (★★★★): Good pals. **3** makes you laugh, and you make them think about how others feel when they're negligently crass or unthinking. You have similar taste in music and the arts, are good for each other's egos, and **3** always makes you see the silly side of your emotional let-downs.

9 and **4** (★★★★): Not a number to excite everyone, you admire **4** as a friend. You see someone who is not necessarily very good at creating their own press; but they are reliable, honest and true in their dealings – all qualities you depend on. Just get them out, sometimes!

9 and **5** (★★★★): This is definitely better as a friendship than a love affair. If you are attracted to each other, you may be lovers for a while and then friends long after – because a **5** has energy and imagination you enjoy, but lacks the reliability you need in business or romantic relationships. Laugh together till late – you're good at that!

8 7 6 5 4 3 2 1 9

9 and **6** (★★★★): Friendship with a **6** may be difficult when you're both feeling sad or oversensitive, and neither wants to hurt the other. But, you want to love **6**, and they are lucky for you in most ways; and, as you're so sociable, you will drag them out when they're feeling low.

9 and **7** (★★): This sets up a chance for the odd clash. You do get on with virtually everyone, but **7** putting their foot right into other people's tender gardens will annoy you. At times, **7** is too blunt, too insensitive; they may offend you, but the conversation can be good, too, and you are certainly both smart. Limit the time you spend together.

9 and **8** (★★★★): This friendship may really work for you. **8** is generous, like you, interested in rational and philosophical thinking, and quite prepared to tell you that you've been wallowing in pity for too long if you have. And, ditto! Good common ground.

9	1	2	3	4	5	6	7	8

9 and **9** (★★): On one hand your **9** friend will be wise and patient with you, understanding your feelings empathetically, sharing your taste. But you can be like glue together, stuck in the same groove and unable to lift each other out. Another **9** may make you see only your negative side.

9 and **11** (★★★★): With both **22**s and **11**s you have a feeling that they are on the same wavelength – and they are. An **11** likes to party but also enjoys good one-on-one contact, and you dream similar dreams. Even the arguments are exciting!

9 and **22** (★★★★): In business or romance, sparks fly. But a **22** is a good playmate for you – perhaps you travel to the same high plain, or visit vibrant cities together. Best joy comes from the way you draw them out when they're overworked – and, when they get those party shoes on, they're fun to be with!

9 IN OTHER PLACES

So what does it mean when your number turns up on a house? Do you live in a 9 home? And how does the number 9 affect your pet – or even the car that you drive? Numbers exude a subtle influence on everything in our lives; and here are just a few examples of how ...

9 1 2 3 4 5 6 7 8

A 9 address

If the number of your address – or of your apartment – reduces back to a **9**, you will have to be a compassionate and charitable person. This is a home in the truest sense – a place of emotional experiences and a haven for friends, and one that may constantly stimulate you to modify it to go along with the mood it has all of its own. This home reflects dreams and possibilities.

As soon as you move in here, leave any prejudice or petty-mindedness behind: only a humanitarian can be happy in a **9** house. Yet is it a place to be lucky, to attract money and good companions, and even the neighbours may be dropping in regularly with a smile and a bottle, hoping they can stay for a chat. Much as you will grow to love it, life will demand that you travel from it and that there will be changes within. People come and go, but it will somehow remain beautiful and calming throughout.

8   7   6   5   4   3   2   1   9

A 9 pet

If you don't know your pet's birthday, use the first letter of their name to calculate their number. If it's an I or an R, they're a **9**. Your **9** pet feels as you do. When your day has been long, or a friend has shouted, or an ex-love has given you a guilty phone call, your **9** pet is there. Sensing things are a little out of joint, the **9** dog places his nose on your lap and pushes to tell you that you have a friend; and the **9** cat jumps up on your lap for a gentle stretch and to purr at you – just to approve of the relationship. Put simply, a **9** pet is your absolute best friend, but they won't accept any barriers between human and quadruped, so make sure you have strong covers on the couch and a rug on the bed.

Maybe the most significant personality trait of your **9** pet is their willingness to travel or move. When you go on holiday, make sure they can come, too – or find them an away-from-home stop which becomes their own weekend break. A **9** pet loves change, and is kind and affable towards everyone – not good if you're hoping for a guard-dog!

A 9 car

If the numbers of your licence plate reduce to **9**, and your car is true to form, everyone will be able to cram into it. Even if it's the smallest model on the market, it will have that personality of largesse and generous room. Your **9** car is going to do a lot of miles, so it seems fitting that it might have a roof rack or a larger-than-average boot; but even if it's a motorbike with a sidecar seat, it will tour!

A **9** vehicle could find its way across the continent without a map, and nothing will keep it from giving its all to tackling the worst weather conditions you can throw at it. Buy it for practicality, but it will soon become a friend you wouldn't dream of parting with – not that it won't prove costly at times, or have moody days. Just roll with it!

YOUR LIFE NUMBER
Your lesson to learn

The time has come to consider the other main
number in your numerology chart: your Life Lesson,
or LIFE, number. This is sometimes also called the
'Birth Force'. Just as for the DAY number, calculating
your LIFE number is easy: simply add together each
digit of your full birth date (day, month and year),
and keep adding the digits until they reduce to a
single number (*see example on page 270*).

*And that's it. You have your Life number.
So what does it tell us?*

9   1   2   3   4   5   6   7   8

What does it mean?

The **LIFE** number takes times to show its mark. You should see its influence over many years, and understand that it is representative of certain strengths and weaknesses that we learn to live with through years of experience. These characteristics need to be analysed over time, and it can take a while for us to come to know ourselves truly from our **LIFE** number. Uncovering these aspects of our character is a process of discovery, and we often don't fully recognize the traits of this number as clearly, or as quickly, as those of the stronger **DAY** number.

Once you have done your sums and discovered this second important number, you'll want to find out what this means. If your **LIFE** and **DAY** numbers are the same, this powerfully reinforces the qualities of your own number, and accentuates both strengths and weaknesses. You won't be fighting corners within your personality by having

8 7 6 5 4 3 2 1 9

two numbers to live with that are, perhaps, miles apart in spirit. But then, equally, if your numbers are the same you may lack a broad vision of the world, seeing with very sharp eyes through just a single (though enormous!) window.

On the following pages we will examine what your **DAY** number **9** is like in tandem with each other number, beginning with the powerful doubling of **9 DAY** and **9 LIFE**, and then moving on through all other possible combinations. If you discover you have a **LIFE** number which totals **11** or **22**, before it reduces to a final single digit of **2** or **4**, read the entry for **9** and **2**, or **9** and **4**, but also pay special attention to any extra information given relating to the added significance of the number being a variation of a master number.

9   1   2   3   4   5   6   7   8

SAME **DAY** AND **LIFE** NUMBER

With two 9s in your number chart, you strive to live an ideal life – and to inspire other people to do the same; you have come into this world prepared for much service and responsibility to others. That said, you come with talents tailored to the cause, for you have a wonderful facility with people and a huge bag of creative and intellectual gifts. You can be as kind to others as Belle is to the Beast, as patient and selfless as Mother Teresa, as astute about the world's future needs as Bill Gates, and as funny and good at getting your point across as Billy Connolly. That's quite a package in one individual, and, if it seems I am overstating the case, the one thing to be truly certain of is that you are a public individual with an urge to perform.

8 7 6 5 4 3 2 1 9

A double **9** is itching for a theatre of some kind – any kind. Even if you are a professional cook, you are bound to entertain as you mash the potatoes, sauté the onions and shave the truffles. Whatever you do, in any field, you do it with flair and a pinch of the unusual, for a double **9** will shy away from a placid and simple life.

Selflessness and compassion for others are at the centre of your life, and a double dose of the number makes you both artist and thinker, perhaps enabling you to step back and gain an impersonal but caring view of the world. This probably means that, on a day-to-day basis, you can see the link between microcosm and macrocosm – how one small issue for an individual has a bearing on a greater issue as it applies more widely. You are adept at seeing something symbolic in the smallest details, and you probably embroider your life in this way, too. Reading a story to a child, for instance, may give you the precise insight you needed to cast off the gloom in a difficult situation of your own. A double **9** understands the great link between all things – and is able to understand the similarities more than the differences.

Double trouble?

If your **LIFE** number total came to '36' before reducing back to the **9**, you have a stronger aspect of determination in your character than many **9**s: you will truly persevere until a task or wish is accomplished. The **9 DAY** energy supports the top number by giving you the grace and humour to survive most crises and see an abstract way of looking at things. And, even when you are forced back a step or two, you will still look for what is good, taking a philosophical stance.

If your total number added to '45', before reducing to **9**, you borrow the energy of the **5** to carry you through the down days that **9**s suffer sometimes, and your intuitive skills are especially sharp. And, if you reached your **9** by first getting a total of '27', your spiritual side is very highly developed, and the **7** adds an extra degree of perfection. You may be hard to please – and find it most difficult to please yourself!

The daily reality of having two birthday **9**s means you're sought out by the crowd: you are *the* hot person to know! Up-to-date on every trend without being a slave to fashion or style, you've read the book before it was a best-seller, seen the film before everyone started talking about it, and have your own opinion, which you will cheerfully expound to others while cooking and quaffing wine. You can't help being entertaining, but you also know what you like, and why. If you can find a way to turn your clever ideas and observations into a business, you will thrive financially and delight in what you do at the same time.

9   1   2   3   4   5   6   7   8

Let me entertain you

A double **9** will have a house with a welcoming front door that is permanently unlatched for friends – and a big dog and good-sized kitchen probably dominate the space, too. **9** has to do everything bigger, but with two **9**s you feel a moral obligation to buy or rent a place big enough to offer accommodation to anyone who might randomly arrive and get a little over-refreshed with the good bottle you've just opened. Others are always in your thinking, but do bear in mind that this can take its toll on a romantic relationship …

9 is so lovable, yet manages to enter a minefield of emotion more of the time than not. Part of the problem is that you can't file your other responsibilities away, so, unless your partner shares one of those **9**s in their birth-day numbers, you may find you push their tolerance to the limit at times. Still, you are forgiving by nature, and adept

8   7   6   5   4   3   2   1   **9**

at manifesting romantic apologies – like a weekend away. And no one can accuse you of being ungenerous – quite the opposite, in fact!

Famous people come and go in your life; you are drawn to – and draw to you – people of the arts and humanities, and they will be impressed by your own breadth of thinking and generosity of spirit. And then, too, there is some elfin quality about you – cheeky humour filtered through a fine mind that is more than sure that unicorns are possible. And, if they are, it is your garden they will visit. A double **9** can make – will make – strange things happen as a matter of course. Would you have it any differently?

DIFFERENT **DAY** AND **LIFE** NUMBERS

Most of us will find that we have two different birthday numbers, and this can be an advantage. One number may soften the single track of the other, and mean we can see other people's viewpoints more easily. At other times, though, the numbers may be in real conflict – and this leads to vacillation in our reactions to everyday situations, or confusion about why we want to run one way and then another.

In the following pages you will discover how your own two numbers are likely to work together, and what you can do to maximize the potential of both when they are paired up.

8 7 6 5 4 3 2 1 9

9 Day with 1 Life

Life has awarded you a very evenly balanced pair of birthday numbers. In a sense, perhaps, nothing could be more desirable than having both a **1** and a **9**, for you can see the start and the end of all things. You have the initial momentum to embark on a plan and the steadiness to see it through, and you show special dramatic flair, which may help kick things off with a bang. You are bound to make a splash in the world.

Your talents are truly diverse, so one problem of this number-pairing is that you often feel torn about which direction to take. You will certainly have big opportunities to show what you're made of, but you can become careless about this, because you expect to do things easily, and to have plenty of invitations in life – both socially and in terms of business propositions. This can cause you to

9   1   2   3   4   5   6   7   8

dissipate your chances, and be led to regret that the **1** makes you more arrogant and feisty than might be wise.

To get the best from both numbers, you need to draw on the self-respect you take from your LIFE number and harness this with the good fellow-feeling you have from DAY **9**. This will make you less likely to offend others, or to feel out of touch with their experiences. **9** is so gifted at knowing how another person is inside, whereas **1** is impatient with folly or perceived weakness. Use the charitable and forgiving side of **9** to offset **1**'s intolerance.

Your LIFE number shows you a world view where anything is possible, and you like to achieve things on your own merits. What you take from **9** is the degree of perfectionism which allows you to reach really significant milestones, and you will also have exactly what it takes to lead the cavalry charge when it comes to any rescue mission – either of an individual person whom you see as oppressed, or of a social cause that needs a champion. You can give tirelessly, and **9** always helps more selfish **1** to see the bigger picture. Fortunately, those tireless energies that come from your **1** give you hope that you really *can* make a difference, whereas **9** alone sometimes feels so sad about the world and the pain in it.

You will have money in your life, and probably some degree of luck in love. Your LIFE number is rather private, and often feels alone and unhelped by anyone, but **9** softens this trait and brings you many friends and admirers. This you usually repay with considerable compassion for others – not always easy for **1** to find!

9   1   2   3   4   5   6   7   8

9 Day with 2 Life

Life has awarded you complementary birthday numbers. Both are feelers, both imaginative, both have a warm heart and a spiritual soul. As a **9 DAY** number dictates the initial direction of your **2** talents, you are likely to travel a great deal, write, speak to many different people and possibly learn a few languages. Your path will not be straight, but it will be eventful and interesting, and you will be known to hundreds – if not thousands.

Your talents are sizeable, and you will have many friends who all have a claim on your time and your affections. **9** makes you romantic, even heroic, and your personal charisma will help you generate interest in matters you think important to spend your time on – quite often, something with a philanthropic tone. But, then, **2** cares deeply for ordinary people, **9** for the whole of humankind,

8 7 6 5 4 3 2 1 9

so you will place a burden on yourself to be sure that your time on earth is well spent. Sometimes, though, your compassionate nature will make extreme demands of you, and with both **2** and **9** colouring your personality you will often become depressed and saddened by others' short-sightedness or bigotry. **9**, though, helps focused **2** become a broader thinker, and allows you time to recover and bounce back from the dramas that can occur in frequent cycles and cause you pain.

In matters of the heart you give your feelings passionately, and ask that your partner does the same, but you have a forgiving side to your nature that **2** by itself sometimes lacks, as **9** can think outside the sense of personal injury. For this reason you are loyal to the one you care for, and a sense of compassion and understanding makes you bigger-hearted than perhaps your partner will be.

The worst attribute of the shyer **2** coming together with **9** is that you may suffer from doubt and vacillation more than you should for someone with your clever mind. **2** can be indecisive at times, and **9** moody, so this energy can undermine your willpower. However, you feel and intuit very acutely what is going on around you, and mostly you will be able to remedy time lost with judicious approaches for a second try. Vocationally, sensitive **2** makes you even better at drama, good with words, and, again, teaching or related professions are natural for you. More than any **2**, don't be surprised if the dominance of the **9** means you will live abroad – or at a distance from your birthplace – for at least some of your life. This will be true even more strongly if the LIFE total reduces to **11** (before the final **2**) – and, in this case, you are likely to find some fame in this world. Or have you already?

9 Day with 3 Life

3 adds the limelight-seeker to **9** the actor, so in some sense your life must be theatrical. You are a great raconteur and can enter into the spirit of other people's stories, dressing the funniest situations in elegant phrases, and laughing heartily at those personal dramas that test you often in your life, no matter how much the laughter belies the pain.

You are philanthropic with a kind outlook on your fellow beings, and, although you are not always able to live up to your personal expectations, you do have a philosophical way of handling disappointment. **3** added to **9** emphasizes your natural degree of compassion and generosity, and you are sympathetic and more selfless than **3** is often given credit for. Because **9** is the mirror number, you entice others to open up to you and show you their

9   1   2   3   4   5   6   7   8

feelings, and are then able to surprise them by reflecting back just what it is that they've said. **3** is often able to illuminate aspects of people's characters in merry ways no one else manages. This talent alone would make you a good writer or dramatist.

By turns, you can be generous and tolerant or critical and demanding. You love to help others, but may be surprised when they put space between you and them, for fear of disappointing you. You don't mean to be bossy, but **9** naturally takes the lead – which is perhaps good for **3**, which sometimes thrashes about to no purpose. Both numbers are emotional, so you may love deeply and be hurt often. Your number **3** helps you to find your own destiny, although **9** has strong issues with the father figure: how will this manifest in your life? Maybe you will seek others whose authority you admire, or perhaps no one will ever live up to your own father; but you have the power to be a good surrogate parent to others, and a skill for seeing something lovely in what others may find almost ugly.

Both numbers give you a beauty and grace of character, and yet each number exacerbates some of the uncertainty of the other. Let others decide on the unimportant things in life – which restaurant to choose, or what colour for a cushion. You are bent on issues concerning what it seems *important* to achieve, and if you utilize your many talents you may be able to direct others' attention to places where it is needed. This number-pairing has the power to show us the way.

9 Day with 4 Life

The forgiving nature led by number **9** softens LIFE **4**'s argumentative character very agreeably. Where **4** can be serious and lack imagination, **9** has excellent humour and a vital idealism about life. With **9** as your main birthday number, you are always searching for greater challenges and more information about the world, **9**'s agile mind compensating for **4**'s occasional slowness in grasping new material. Where **4** will painstakingly sift through many details and form an opinion, **9** has an instant overview of the facts, and will assess a situation or a relationship largely intuitively. This is a blessing for **4**, although you gain a sense of reason from **4** which is never compromised.

And lest **9** feel – as so often – that achievements can come easily and without effort, your **4** ethic of earning what you get prevents such presumptive habits from taking

8   7   6   5   4   3   2   1   9

root. This is excellent, because **9** has considerable talent in drama and the arts, and **4** understands very well the grind that is required to elicit something tangible from such talent. Success in such fields is much more certain from the combination of these two numbers.

9 often suffers many disappointments in life, especially concerning family during their upbringing. An anchoring number like **4** lends **9** vital stoicism, and allows a greater sense of security to develop even in adversity. In other words, though as a **9** you experience and feel other's pain, as a **4** you understand how to shape a sensible attitude from this, and survive each drama. **9** is also a talented dreamer and a philanthropist, but through the number **4** you add a rational expression to such thinking and find practical ways to improve the situations that trouble you. **9** and **4** might well persuade each other into governmental or agency jobs which demand the concern for a large number of people.

9	1	2	3	4	5	6	7	8

Perhaps what is best of all, **9** gifts **4** with imagination, generosity and empathy – the very things most likely to be missed in **4**'s overall make-up. In short, these two numbers offer each other enough talent and elements of character to cover a much broader canvas over a lifetime – and with many and varied subtle colours.

9 Day with 5 Life

9 is the last number, so you will always feel the push to see things through to the end. This is such an asset for a restless LIFE **5**, who often picks up a thousand different things and never finishes one of them. You really have the ability to take a fantastical project and see it through to completion – and that is a gift for a **5** birthday number. However, just as **9** is good at so many things, so is **5**! You may bite off an awful lot to chew on, and could find it hard to decide what direction you are going to take with your life, as you excel so easily at such a diverse range of things.

5 is a party animal, seen at all the social events and desired by all who meet them. Yet **9** has a depth behind **5**'s vibrant personality, making you acutely aware of what support other people need. **9** always picks the perfect present and has an eye for the unusual, ensuring the gift will

9   1   2   3   4   5   6   7   8

be talked about for years. **LIFE 5**, though, is such an exciting number that really creates sunshine around you, and **9**'s extraordinary people skills mean that this pairing brings out the sunshine in everyone else as well. **9** is charitable and forgiving even when **5** is rash and hot-headed, but **5**'s affability makes **9**'s offers of charity easily acceptable. **9** mellows **5**'s constant energy, and gives the rambunctious number clearer vision in the face of adversity, while **5** enables gloomy **9** to smile more often.

9 attracts friends and admirers, which the sexy **5** then handles to perfection: you leave a path of fascination in your wake! Yet love is not always easy for the determined but tempestuous **5**, who is so adored by so many (too many?). **9** is the diplomat for **5**, helping you to be seen by those around you as the person you really are; the image that others have formed of the intoxicating but also exasperating **5** needs such a partner number. Everyone wants a piece of **5** – their style, their humour and their infectious attitude towards life. Sensible, well-mannered **9** offsets this shallow image of **5**, and makes you accessible and more beloved, helping you to see a bigger picture.

Your **9 DAY** number adds generosity and compliance, while **LIFE 5** reminds you to keep some time for your own energetic and sensuous needs. While **9** alone would simply buy an adventure holiday for their friends, **5** makes you take the holiday yourself – and ensures that you have the fetching beachwear to get you noticed at the same time! Have fun with the **5** side of your nature, and don't always allow **9** to be the giver but never the recipient. As **5** would say, life is for the living and not just the giving.

9 Day with 6 Life

Being the last number of the cycle, any number-pairing with **9** usually means that you are good at seeing things through to a conclusion, and this is very important for multi-talented **6**, who can so easily get lost in the labyrinth of things that they are good at. With a **6 LIFE** number, **9**'s sometimes depressive or reclusive tendencies are swept away and replaced by **6**'s trademark geniality. But then, **9** adds practicality to **6**'s skill, and gives a different depth to the easy-going **6**, too.

With the beauty of number **6** on your side, you are bound to succeed at anything you turn your hand to. **9**s and **6**s both have the friends, the social invitations and all the good humour to ensure you get meetings with the right people to help you to your purpose. **DAY** number **9** gifts the necessary vision that makes your **6** dreams of a

8   7   6   5   4   3   2   1   9

beautiful life a reality, making excellent use of your serious artistic skills. **9** envisages an end use for the diverse range of talents that **6** is good at. **9** can demonstrate extraordinary people skills itself, being a good public speaker and 'big brother' figure to everyone; but **6** is the gentle yet upbeat other half it needs. **9**'s sometimes critical, and silently severe, opinions are partially calmed by **6**'s forgiving nature, making you a really lovely, charitable person.

Relationships are not always the easiest thing for a **9/6**, as both numbers bring numerous friends and admirers, but possibly no one you would trust your heart to. And **6**'s occasionally shy behaviour is allowed to run riot a little by **9** – not known for its vivacity. Whereas **6** can be so stubborn, headstrong and demanding when provoked, **9** is more flexible, and quietens these hidden demons, making you an easy-going friend. But don't let **9**'s mildness stop you from expressing your emotions now and again, and don't become trapped in a dutiful/reliable role with some-

9   1   2   3   4   5   6   7   8

one, when you would naturally prefer to give rein to a sexier, more sultry persona with a racy heart!

9 is wise, and this diminishes the amount of secret complaining and perceived frustration that a number **6** feels entitled to – offering new perspective on everything ... although, with **6** as your LIFE number, there is no doubt that your generous nature will usually win out eventually anyway. But **9** pulls the sometimes stay-at-home **6** out into the world more, and, with creative and musical talents up to your armpits, you are certain to be a success at what you do. But don't let your **6** LIFE number mean that you wait for good things to come to you!

9 Day with 7 Life

The mixing of these numbers witnesses **9** colouring **7**'s specialized artistry with dramatic flavours and textures. **7** looks beneath the surface to know what another person is thinking; **9** feels as they are feeling. Given the blend of these two numbers, then, drama and writing are possible vocations for a **9/7** to take. What is interesting, though, is that this combination intensifies the idealism inherent in both numbers, so the influence of **9** makes the most romantic version of a LIFE **7** imaginable. **7**'s dignity and elegance also vivifies **9**'s already considerable personal magnetism, so we are looking at quite an impressive teaming of numbers.

With **9** urging you to get on with a broader group of friends, **7**'s antithesis to larger gatherings is somewhat smoothed over: **9** helps **7** overcome what is a mixture of

9	1	2	3	4	5	6	7	8

shyness and pride to let its real inner warmth be felt by others. **9** also makes a huge impact on the level of **7**'s physical energy, enticing you to get out and join in life at the actual rather than the cerebral level. **7** can be very reserved, but **9** is gregarious and sociable. This makes the sharp **7** humour more palatable and, though your critical element never leaves you behind, whatever you say probably comes out with a blend of archness and sweetness that makes it impossible for anyone to take offence. **9** is also very responsible, and this, too, steers **7** away from that tendency to stay out of other people's affairs because it seems ill-mannered to intrude. With **9** and **7** together, you will often intrude – and will be heartily thanked for it.

In women, discerning **7** makes more of a sexy lioness out of charming **9**. You will leave that distinctive lipstick mark on your wine glass, which fills in a hundred unspoken words to the lover you are quarrelling with. The parting jibe is unnecessary, as **9** has dramatic flair and **7** the cool authority to leave the room in total control. And the next day you'll be bombarded with messages and apologies – and *you* will decide when to answer them. This is because **9**'s sense of the broader picture helps **7** get out of that hurt place where it might otherwise just retire to lick its wounds.

One interesting manifestation of **9** and **7** within one individual is that, for all that beauty and nobility of character, there is a disconcerting lack of certainty in what you do. You may be timid when others least expect it from you, or you may vacillate and become moody, and refuse to clinch an option or an opportunity. At times, these delays are very costly. Just remember that your numbers married together blend exceptional style and taste with a deep feeling for how to turn unlovely things into lovelier ones. Believe in yourself more, for there's no doubt that everyone else does!

9   1   2   3   4   5   6   7   8

9 Day with 8 Life

A **LIFE 8** with a **DAY** number of **9** will be a wise old owl! Already humorous, **9** gets an extra pinch of wit from **8**, which assures not only that your peers pay you homage for your excellent mind and aura of knowledge, but also that they hang on your every word. The bon mot is a daily occurrence from you, and you will find yourself requited over and again. Perhaps perfect life would see you writing the headlines for the newspaper you already own!

A **DAY** number of **9** allows you to feel very deeply for other people, but you can sometimes be impressionable and take on too many of life's responsibilities. This is where **LIFE 8** comes in and avoids calamity, for, although **8** is always willing to be all things to everyone, its organizational expertise allows you to take control more dispassionately. A female **8**, for instance, howls with agony if a

stocking ladders or a nail breaks, but if someone has a rup-
tured artery or falls down the stairs and breaks a leg, they
can handle it without missing a beat. This is vital for **DAY
9**, always participating in the pain, and that raft of security
that is deep within an **8**'s character helps you overcome
the disappointments **9**s so often have thrust upon them.
Your **DAY** number is guilty of enticing you to give to other
people to the point of personal detriment, but, oddly
enough, **8** sees all and keeps things in check.

So, a **9/8** will have both a perceptive and a practical
mind (thanks to **8**) and intelligent eloquence (thanks to **9**).
These combined talents surely see you shimmy your way
up the pole of achievement. You may be attracted to per-
forming arts or government work, because these two
numbers together suddenly become very public and flirt
with fame. Or, literature and other forms of writing – even
dramatic, since **9** is so strongly concerned with drama and
film – may be your overwhelming desire. In any field, **8** has

the nous and **9** the raw talent to make any competitors feel like amateurs. Both numbers together also make you more sexy, sultry and secretive.

In short, **9** has the flair to sashay down the street with a warm and friendly outward manner that attracts comment and admiration from passers-by; **8** helps you do this with heels on. Both numbers are travelling – up, out, away. Nothing stays stagnant, and no goal remains the only goal, when you dance to the beat of these two numbers. A great host or hostess, with a busy, delving mind, you will make others breathless watching what you get though in a month. That would be another's lifetime!

THE FUTURE
Take a look what's in store...

And now we come to the calculation of your future.
Each year, on your birthday, you move into a new
sphere of number-influence which governs that year.
The numbers progress in cycles of nine years; after
nine years, the cycle starts over again, and a whole
new period of your life begins afresh. The cycle can
be applied to every number, so you can discover what
the main issues will be for partners, friends and
family, as well as for yourself, in any given year (*see
calculation instructions, opposite*). Emphasis is placed
on what will happen to you when you are in your
own year number – that is, in any '9' year cycle.

9 1 2 3 4 5 6 7 8

Working out your cycle

To find out what year you're currently in, use the same formula employed for calculating the LIFE number, but substitute the current year for the year in which you were born. Every year, the cycle then moves on by one more number until, after a **9** year, returning to **1**, to begin the cycle again.

Calculation example 1

BIRTHDAY: 18 February 1962

TO CALCULATE THE
CURRENT YEAR NUMBER:
$1+8+2+\left[\underbrace{2+0+0+7}_{\text{CURRENT YEAR}}\right] = 20$, and $2+0 = $ **2**

*This means that on 18 February 2007 you move into a **2** year. On 18 February the following year, this would then move into a **3** year (1+8+2+2+0+0+8 = 21, and 2+1 = **3**), and the year after that, a **4** year, and so on.*

8	7	6	5	4	3	2	1	9

Calculation example 2

BIRTHDAY: 27 August 1981

TO CALCULATE THE CURRENT YEAR NUMBER: $2+7+8+\left[\underbrace{2+0+0+7}_{\text{CURRENT YEAR}}\right]$ = 26, and 2+6 = **8**

This means that on 27 August 2007 you move into an **8** *year. On 27 August the following year, this would then move into a* **9** *year (2+7+8+2+0+0+8 = 27, and 2+7 =* **9***), and the year after that, a* **1** *year, and so on.*

Many numerologists feel that the impact of a year number can be felt from the first day of that year – in other words, from 1st January. However, the usual school of thought is that the new number cycle is initiated *on your birthday itself*, and my experience tends to corroborate this. So, if your birthday is fairly late in the year – November or December, say – this means that you will have gone through most of the calendrical year before *your* new

9   1   2   3   4   5   6   7   8

number-year cycle for that year begins.

Look back over some recent years, and see if – in the descriptions on the following pages – you can pinpoint the moment when your yearly number-cycle for any given year became apparent. You'll be amazed at just how accurate this system seems to be.

8   7   6   5   4   3   2   1   9

A 1 year

This is the perfect time to set up new and quite specific long-term goals, and consider just where you want to be a few years from now. You will have new people around you from this point on, and fresh ideas about them and the interests they awaken in you. This is a completely new chapter in your life, and you should set goals for a better and more fulfilling future.

Career-wise, a **1** year often occurs at a time of new employment, or of a complete change in direction in your working life. You are probably wanting to develop new skills or make use of untested talents. You have to believe in yourself now. This is the time when it's a little easier to step back and see how to get started along a particular path. Goals, you will understand, are perfectly attainable, even if a year ago they seemed unrealistic. In a **1** year you have tremendous focus and independence, and excellent determination.

The secret to your success now is in your ability to concentrate; but, emotionally, things can be quite testing. No matter how strong a love bond may be in your life, a **1** year demands that you do much for yourself. You could feel isolated or unsupported, even if someone dear is close by. This is a test of your own courage and inner strength. Only your strongest desires will gain results ... but then, your desires should be fierce during this cycle. Try not to act impulsively, as the push to do so will be powerful, but also, don't be afraid to be independent and go your own way. Strong urges are driving you – forward, for the most part – and a **1** year lends you exceptional clarity and energy.

8   7   6   5   4   3   2   1   9

A 2 year

A year which demands co-operation and partnerships at every level, **2** is a gentle year cycle, when you can consolidate what you started in the previous twelve months. You will need to be diplomatic and sensitive towards other people's feelings, but your intuition is very strong now, and you are able to share the load and the initiative more than you were allowed last year. For this reason, don't try to push things too far or too fast. After the previous whirlwind year, this is a moment to take your time and get things right.

Relationships come more into focus during a **2** year. This is especially pleasing if someone new entered your life in the last year or so, for the vibration of **2** helps a bond to strengthen, and a feeling of mutuality improves now. In some ways you may feel the desire or the need to

9   1   2   3   4   5   6   7   8

be secretive, but this is because there are unknown elements at work all on fronts. It will affect you at work and at play, and in a close tie you will discover new tenderness that will probably separate you from other friends. If there is no one special currently in your life, this may be the year to find someone: a **2** year brings a relationship much stronger than a fling!

Your negotiation skills and ability to guess what another person is feeling may work very well for you this year; and, if the number **2** derives from master number **11** (which it almost surely will), there is a chance for serious partnerships and master opportunities. You will need to look at contracts carefully, and spend time on legalities. But this is often the most exciting and unusual year out of the nine. Mysteries come to light, and your ideas flow well. Just be prepared to consider another person in every equation.

A 3 year

Time for you! This twelve-month period is concerned with developing your abilities and testing your flexibility. Your imagination is especially strong, and you may have particular opportunities to improve your wealth and make lasting friendships. You will also need to be focused, because the energy of a **3** year is fast and furious, and may make you feel dissolute. Usually, though, this is a happy year spent with some travel prospects and many creative inspirations. Difficulties which intruded in the previous two years are often resolved in this year cycle.

Business and your social life often run together in a **3** year, and work will be a lot of fun. It is worth taking time over your appearance and indulging yourself more than usual, for the sociability of this number brings you many invitations and a chance to create a new look, or to explore

9   1   2   3   4   5   6   7   8

other aspects of your personality. You have extra charm this year, so try to use it where it is needed.

Many people find that the number **3** expresses itself in a year cycle as a third person to consider: frequently, this is the birth of a child or an addition to the family, but it might be that another party pressures you in your personal relationship. Don't talk too much about this, or show nervousness. Under a **3** vibration, it is easy to become exhausted – even through over-excitement – so be alert to the impulse towards extravagance and fragmentation. Try to enjoy the way in which you are being drawn out of yourself this year, and allow yourself time to study, write, paint. Anything you really want you can achieve now – even strange wishes and desires can be pulled towards you. Make sure you think a little about what you are asking for!

A 4 year

A much-needed year of good-housekeeping – on the personal level, as well as literally. This year will demand practicality from you. Often a **4** brings a focus on money or accounts, on repairs around the home, or on putting your life into better order. It may not be what you want, yet it will force itself upon you. It is sometimes a year spent with a pen in hand – writing lists or cheques, doing sums and keeping diaries. It is also a year when you will need to do some research, to find out about what you don't know.

You have so much work to do in a **4**, or **22**, year – more than for a long time. Your personal pleasure takes second place to requirement, and it may seem difficult to stick to the task sometimes. Money demands that you do so, for extra expenditure is not advised in this twelve-month period. Yet if this sounds stressful, it also gives you a feeling of satisfaction that you will achieve so much this year – a job of hard work and dedication really well done. It may be that this year gives you a very good foundation for the future and sets up lasting improvements.

You will never survive a **4** – or, especially, a **22** – year if you are not organized and implement a system of work and life. Be honest in what you do with others, but also in what you do for yourself. You cannot deceive yourself, and must check details carefully. You may have a feeling of burden at times, but there is a chance to feel you have done something extraordinary, too. Translate your clever ideas into practical results. The most significant thing for you to do is to concentrate on proper personal management. The weight of the world is on your shoulders, but you can bear it if the preparations you make are good. There is no escape from demands on your time and intelligence, but nothing can be hurried, so face the job ahead and you will soon find you have climbed a hill to new vistas.

8   7   6   5   4   3   2   1   9

A 5 year

After careful management of your time last year, and a feeling of being tied to the wheel, this will seem like bursting from the inside of a darkened room into bright light. Now you have a change from routine to madness, and you may feel a personal freedom that was denied you last year. Nevertheless, nothing is completely settled in a **5** year, and this uncertainty may take its toll. Try to look at this cycle as a chance to find success in newer areas, and a way to advance from necessary stagnation into running waters of energy and vitality. You will update your sense of yourself during this period, and make progress towards the life you want, following the previous year's required self-discipline.

You are admitting to the need for new pastures, so your ideas of what your life might include, or who may have a role in it, may alter now. No one likes to be held back in

9   1   2   3   4   5   6   7   8

a **5** year, but it is still important not to be too hasty in your actions. Use your energies, by all means, but govern them with your head. This is the time for innovation, and new takes on old goals, but if you quarrel with those dear to you, or with whom you work, it may be difficult to repair later. If change is still inevitable, be as kind and constructive as possible, and make sure you aren't leaping from one difficult situation straight into another. You need to discover your versatility and personal resourcefulness to get the best out of this cycle. And, for some of the twelve months, travel or lots of movement seems inescapable.

This year is potentially some kind of turning point for you. Learning how to adapt to sudden circumstances is vital, because any plans or directives set in stone will cause you pain, and possibly come unstuck. Be prepared for changes and, if this brings a nervousness with it, try to meet the adventure head-on. If you talk yourself up and take on a front-running position, you can work wonders in a **5** year.

8 7 6 5 4 3 2 1 9

A 6 year

Love is in the air. Other things seize your time too – your home needs attention, and duties demand your energy – but, principally, this year is about emotions and relationships. Sometimes love and happiness are a reward for surviving so much in the past two years, and for unselfish service and support for others. The emphasis is on finding harmony with others, and this may come in various ways. This year, you may have the impetus and opportunity to erase problems that have previously beset you. You understand, and feel acutely sensitive towards, others, and are more radiant and beautiful than you have been for some time. If you can be kind and positive in emotional dealings, you will benefit in many ways, including materially.

There are hurdles in a **6** year in connection with obligations you feel towards others. At times you are stretched,

9   1   2   3   4   5   6   7   8

because there are personal desires and ties you want to nurture which are countermanded by the duties you are subjected to. You may resent this, yet, if you can remain cheerful, you will be rewarded in ways not immediately apparent. Love is trying to sweep you off your feet, but your health may suffer because you are trying to fit in so much, and the intensity of your feelings is strong.

While it's good to be helpful in a **6** year, don't allow yourself to be taken advantage of, or let people drain you completely. Set up a system that lets you delegate some responsibility. Your home may bloom while you're in such a happy mood, and you should feel creative and mellow. The events of a **6** year are not as fast and furious as the previous year, but things move steadily towards a happier state of being. Let the time go as it will, because this is not a year to fight against what comes to you; get into the right philosophical gear and open yourself to pleasant surprises that come from being useful, and being warm with others.

A 7 year

This year is a time for manifesting your goals by visualizing them. See yourself triumphing and continuing toward your vision. Never lose sight of what you want, or confusion will reign. You'll be tempted this way and that, annoyed by gossip, and attacked by those who love you but don't understand what you are trying to do. Don't be swayed by them, or you will lose your opportunities and precious time.

Keep your head, as everything depends on your state of mind. Refuse to react to distractions, and avoid hasty actions or sudden decisions. A calm approach is the best remedy to the chaos surrounding you. You may have to move house without warning, but take it in your stride and make a calm, clear choice on where to go. If you are travelling somewhere exotic, be prepared with vitamins

9   1   2   3   4   5   6   7   8

and medicines to avoid viruses of any kind.

Legal matters may arise during this year, relating to business, investments or house options. Consult an expert to avoid pitfalls, and, when you feel happy, proceed with confidence. If you have taken all the facts and details into account, you'll now be within sight of your goal. But watch your health, as the number 7 is connected with this subject for both good and ill. You might get fit and lose some weight or, conversely, suffer with some little grievance. This is a time for mental, spiritual and physical detoxing. Also, rest: take a vacation to the country, to a quiet location where you can think in peace. Let no one confuse you. You may have to wait, but you will know how to come out on top if you listen to your intuition.

This is an excellent year for study, research, writing and reading, and clearing out all the unnecessary people or ideas from your past.

8 7 6 5 4 3 2 1 9

An 8 year

This cycle brings the possible finding of a soulmate. If you're single, you could not have a better chance of meeting that special someone than now. **8** years also relate to money, so you may be caught up with an impossible workload and regard the arrival of such a potentially strong love as poor timing – and perhaps this is why it comes to you, because your attention being taken up elsewhere may be the best reason for someone's admiration. The love vibration you experience under karmic year number **8** may point to a future relationship prospect which has a lasting importance.

For those in settled relationships, pregnancy sometimes comes with this number, and it brings a very special link between the child and their parents. Or, you may experience a deep urge to study a subject that comes easily to you, though you have never learned about it before – a

9   1   2   3   4   5   6   7   8

language, perhaps, or an artistic skill you were attracted to but never developed, but which you now pick up well. Even a professional subject that you seem to grasp quickly will seem more important to perfect than ever before. Partly, this is because **8** year cycles concern making more money, and dealing with the deeply felt past. There are huge opportunities for you in an **8** year, and you will want to be prepared to maximize them. However, you'll need to use good judgement and be efficient with your time management.

Many people feel pushed to the limit in an **8** year, because there is just so much going on. Consider, though, that the vibration of the number wants to find positive expression, so the more efficiency and determination you can bring to it, the better the chance of finishing on a high note. Don't over-commit your time or money, and be ready to acquiesce to others' ways of doing things. You need to be confident, but ready to adjust too. **8** is made up of two circles, asking 'infinity' of you. But this year, you can do it!

8   7   6   5   4   3   2   1   9

A 9 year

Your personal affairs all come to a head in a **9** year, and whatever has been insufficient, or unsatisfying, will rise to the surface and demand change now. It could be the fulfilment of many dreams, for this is the culmination of nine years' experience. Whatever is jettisoned was probably no longer of use – though this might seem dispassionate. Many friendships will drift away, but you have probably outgrown them. The strongest demand of you is a readiness to discard what will not be part of your serious future – and this can mean a temporary feeling of insecurity.

You will certainly travel in a **9** year. Even if a trip is short, or of no great distance, it will settle something in your mind. The more compassionate, tolerant and forgiving you are, the more warmth and generosity will come to you. This is not the right moment to start something com-

| 9 | 1 | 2 | 3 | 4 | 5 | 6 | 7 | 8 |

pletely new, but if events arise as a natural conclusion to what has gone before, this is a good thing. Your mind needs to engage with bigger issues, for selfishness or petty ideas will cause you unhappiness under this number. People will thwart you in your career and personal matters – and these obstacles seem to come out of the blue, and are beyond your control. However, if you think on philosophical issues and remain open to big ideas, everything will turn out well.

A **9** year can be populated with many friends and activities, yet can feel lonely too; this is a cycle for completion of tasks and the ending of what is not enduring. But this is the right time to see the fruits of previous work. Be wise about where your destiny seems to want to take you. Your artistic and imaginative facilities are inspired now, and you'll begin to see new directions that you must investigate in the years ahead. You know what is missing in your life, or where you've failed yourself, and can now – in your own year cycle – prepare for the adventure about to dawn.

8   7   6   5   4   3   2   1   9

How to find your DAY NUMBER

Add the digits for the day of birth, and keep adding them until they reduce to one number:

EXAMPLES

18 February 1962	1+8 = **9**
27 August 1981	2+7 = **9**

How to find your LIFE NUMBER

Add the digits for the day, month and year of birth, and keep adding them until they reduce to one number:

EXAMPLES

18 February 1962	1+8+2+1+9+6+2 = 29
	2+9 = 11 (a 'master' number), and 1+1 = **2**
27 August 1981	2+7+8+1+9+8+1 = 36,
	and 3+6 = **9**

Further reading

The Complete Book of Numerology, David A. Phillips, Hay House, 2006

The Day You Were Born: A Journey to Wholeness Through Astrology and Numerology, Linda Joyce, Citadel Press, 2003

Many Things on Numerology, Juno Jordan, De Vorss Books, 1981

Numerology, Hans Decoz and Tom Monte, Perigee Books, 2001

Numerology: The Romance in Your Name, Juno Jordan, De Vorss Books, 1977

Sacred Number, Miranda Lundy, Wooden Books, 2006

The Secret Science of Numerology: The Hidden Meaning of Numbers and Letters, Shirley Blackwell Lawrence, New Page Books, 2001

About the author

Titania Hardie is Britain's favourite 'Good Witch' and a best-selling author. Born in Sydney, Australia, Titania has a degree in English and Psychology, and also trained in parapsychology and horary astrology. With a high media profile, she regularly appears on television in the UK, US, Canada, Australia and South Africa, as well as receiving widespread newspaper and magazine coverage. Her previous titles have sold over a million copies worldwide, and include *Titania's Crystal Ball*, *Aroma Magic*, and *Hocus Pocus*. Her first novel is due to be published in summer 2007.

Acknowledgements

Many thanks to you, Nick, for the clear and brilliant vision; you knew what you wanted and, like a true and inspired **1**, kept mulling it over until a way was found. This is your baby. Also big thanks to Tessa, master number **22**, for your commitment to this magnum opus beyond call: only you and I know, Tessa, how much time and soul has gone into all of these words. To Ian, for keeping us piping along with a true **4**'s sanguine approach to such a long body of work, and to Elaine and Malcolm for the look – **6**s, naturally! For my daughter Samantha, thanks for some of your ideas which found expression in the second-to-last section: I love the latte in Soho while signing the author. Let's see! To Georgia, for work in the field on number **5**, my thanks. To all of you, my appreciation, and I wish you all LUCKY NUMBERS!

EDDISON·SADD EDITIONS

Editorial Director Ian Jackson
Managing Editor Tessa Monina
Proofreader Nikky Twyman

Art Director Elaine Partington
Mac Designer Karen Watts
Production Sarah Rooney